The Pennsylvania Tradition
of Semitics
A Century of Near Eastern
and Biblical Studies
at the University of Pennsylvania

SOCIETY OF BIBLICAL LITERATURE
BIBLICAL SCHOLARSHIP IN NORTH AMERICA

Kent Harold Richards, Editor

The Pennsylvania Tradition of Semitics

of Semitics

A Century of Near Eastern
and Biblical Studies
at the University of Pennsylvania

by

CYRUS H. GORDON
New York University

Scholars Press
Atlanta, Georgia

SOCIETY OF BIBLICAL LITERATURE
CENTENNIAL PUBLICATIONS

Editorial Board

The Society of Biblical Literature gratefully acknowledges a grant from the National Endowment for the Humanities to underwrite certain editorial and research expenses of the Centennial Publications Series. Published results and interpretations do not necessarily represent the view of the Endowment.

Library of Congress Cataloging-in-Publication Data

Gordon, Cyrus Herzl, 1908–
The Pennsylvania tradition of semitics.

(Biblical scholarship in North America ; no. 13)
1. Semitic philology—Study and teaching (Higher)—
Pennsylvania—Philadelphia.   2. Near East—Study and
teaching (Higher)—Pennsylvania—Philadelphia.   3. Bible
—Study—Pennsylvania—Philadelphia.   4. University of
Pennsylvania.   I. Title.   II. Series.
PJ3013.U55G67   1986   492′.07′1174811   86-28005
ISBN 1-55540-022-1 (alk. paper)
ISBN 1-55540-023-X (pbk. : alk. paper)

TABLE OF CONTENTS

INTRODUCTION

Parts of the story I am about to tell are more personal than others. Some sections are intimate, while others are formal, depending on whether my information is firsthand, or archival.[1] As a disciple, I can describe my teacher James A. Montgomery and his courses with some insight. But I cannot do comparable justice to all of the current faculty and their subjects, on account of limited acquaintance. I trust the following paragraphs will explain both my competence and my insufficiencies.

As a native Philadelphian interested in Semitics since my high school days, I was fortunate to live near the campus of the University of Pennsylvania, where I received my undergraduate and doctoral training between 1924 and 1930. I then taught Hebrew and Assyrian at my alma mater during the years 1930–31.

Then, as now, the American Schools of Oriental Research in Jerusalem and Baghdad had close ties with the University of Pennsylvania and its University Museum. Between 1931 and 1935, as a Fellow of the American Schools of Oriental Research on joint expeditions in Iraq and Palestine, I remained in close contact with my former teachers and colleagues at Penn.

From 1946 to 1956, as Professor of Assyriology and Egyptology at Dropsie College in Philadelphia, I was close to the University of Pennsylvania scene and participated in the monthly sessions of the Philadelphia Oriental Club on the Penn campus.

[1] The archives of the University of Pennsylvania library contain a set of the catalogues. The titles of the latter have gradually changed since the beginnings in the 1880s. For example in 1890–91, the title was *University of Pennsylvania, Catalogue and Announcement (1890–91)*. In 1894, the title was modified to *Catalogue of University of Pennsylvania 1894–1895*. With the advent of graduate studies, in the *University of Pennsylvania Catalogue* of 1906–07, there was a *Fasciculus of the Graduate School* containing *Announcements for* [e.g.] *1907–08*. Eventually there was a separate graduate catalogue, e.g., *University of Pennsylvania, Graduate School 1915–16*. By 1983 there were two large and separate publications: the *University of Pennsylvania Bulletin 1982–83, Undergraduate Courses of Study*, and *University of Pennsylvania Bulletin, Information for Graduate Studies 1982–83*. The current scene is chronicled in three Penn catalogues: *PENN: Undergraduate Academic Bulletin 1983–1985, PENN: Graduate Academic Bulletin 1983–1985*, and *PENN: Graduate Admissions Catalogue 1985–1987*.

There are some observations of interest for Semitic and oriental studies in Edward Potts Cheyney, *History of the University of Pennsylvania 1740–1940* (Philadelphia: University of Pennsylvania Press, 1940), 134, 350; and in Cornell M. Dowlin (ed.), *The University of Pennsylvania Today, Bicentennial Celebration 1740–1940* (Philadelphia: University of Pennsylvania Press), 84.

So, for quite a few years, spanning four decades, I was part of, or close to, the University and its Semitics program. It is understandable that the years during which I was part of the scene will be treated more intimately than those before and after. However, I heard so much during the twenties and thirties from my mentor, Professor Montgomery, about the "good old days," which he remembered from the beginnings of Oriental Studies at Penn in the 1880s, that I feel almost as though I had lived through them myself.

Though Semitics at Penn, as elsewhere, has undergone steady modification down to the present, my alma mater endures as a major teaching, research, and publication center of Semitics and Near Eastern studies, respected throughout the world of learning.

I owe a debt of gratitude to Professor and Mrs. Svi Rin for facilitating my archival studies, to Professor Jeffrey Tigay for valuable notes on Hebraica and Judaica at Penn, to Professor Åke Sjöberg for showing me the inner workings of the Sumerian Dictionary Project, to Associate Professor William Hanaway for arranging a meeting with him and other members of the Department of Oriental Studies faculty, and to Mrs. Edith Creter not only for typing my manuscript but also for catching many a slip.

Cyrus H. Gordon
Brookline, MA
18 September 1985

1. THE BEGINNINGS

The concern of Western civilization with Semitics stems from the importance of the Old Testament for Christendom. Early Church Fathers such as Origen (third century A.D.) were expert in the text of the Hebrew Bible and made it more accessible to Greek Christian scholars. As the center of gravity for Christendom moved toward the Latin West, it became evident to savants such as Jerome (died A.D. 420) that a control of Hebrew, Greek, and Latin constituted the necessary tools for anyone who aspired to enlightenment founded on primary sources. After years of serious study and research, Jerome could rightly boast of being a *Hebraeus* as well as a *Graecus* and *Latinus*. A *Latinus* was not synonymous with a *Romanus* (a Roman); instead, it meant one conversant with the Latin language, literature and values. By the same token, Jerome the *Graecus* was not a Greek, but a master of the Greek language with the means of penetrating the messages of Greek texts. Similarly, *Hebraeus*, unlike *Judaeus* (Jew), designated a scholar of Hebrew writings. To become a *Hebraeus*, Jerome migrated to Palestine where he studied under learned rabbis.

Ever since the days of Jerome, there has been an elite in Christendom cherishing the combination of Latin, Greek, and Hebrew as the humanistic basis of a real education. During the Renaissance and Reformation, what was to grow into oriental (Near Eastern) studies hinged on the study of the Hebrew Bible, the Talmud, the kabbalah and other rabbinic texts.

The eighteenth century (during which the University of Pennsylvania was founded) is aptly called the Enlightenment. It was an age of intellectual curiosity and discovery. Human minds and horizons were expanding. Explorations into the East embraced, for example, Iran, where copies of the royal Achaemenian inscriptions were made with sufficient care to make possible the decipherment of cuneiform in the nineteenth century. Moreover, in the eighteenth century, the study of Near Eastern languages spread beyond Hebrew to embrace Arabic, Syriac, and Coptic.

Early in the eighteenth century (1709), formal excavations at Herculaneum began; later, in 1748, they were begun also at nearby Pompeii. Both towns had been destroyed in A.D. 79 by an eruption of Mount Vesuvius. Thus, the University of Pennsylvania was founded (in 1740) at the time of sensational excavations that foreshadowed the age of field archaeology. The latter was to make Semitic studies at Penn famous, albeit after a lag of about 150 years.

Another development in the eighteenth century was crucial in shaping Semitics at Penn. Britain had wrested India from the Mogul emperors, and some talented British went there with sharp minds worthy of the Enlightenment. Among them was Sir William Jones (1746–94), who learned Sanskrit, the classical language of India, and observed that Sanskrit was linguistically related to Greek, Latin, and familiar languages in Western Europe. This was the birth of what we now call comparative Indo-European linguistics. In the nineteenth century, continental European scholars (mainly Germans like Jacob Grimm, 1785–1863) demonstrated that the correspondences of sounds in the same words, as they changed from language to language, followed exact laws; this was to become the backbone of what we now call linguistic science. Although scientific linguistics started with Indo-European, it spread to the study of Semitics and eventually to the serious study of every language.

Benjamin Franklin (1706–90) was one of the great spirits of the Enlightenment. As an American, he had not been exposed to the classical literary heritage as it was fostered among the intellectuals of Europe. But in curiosity, reasoning, originality, and scientific achievement, he stands out among the leaders of the Enlightenment at home and abroad. In 1740 he founded the College of Philadelphia, soon to become known as the University of Pennsylvania. It was the first college in colonial America founded on strictly secular principles; thus, it had no divinity school. The usual American pattern, starting with Harvard in 1636, called for the establishment of a college or university under the auspices of a specific Protestant denomination. By excluding theology, Franklin predetermined that when the University of Pennsylvania came of age and would have a Semitics department, it would be in accordance with the standards of two sciences, yet to be born: archaeology and linguistics;[1] but theology would not influence its development. However, this important precedent carried with it a disadvantage. It was difficult to include Hebrew (and therefore Semitics) in the curriculum, whereas the denominationally oriented universities could offer Hebrew instruction without hindrance from the start. This limitation at Penn was more serious than might meet the eye. A sizable proportion of the student body planned to enter the Protestant ministry, and in those days, any divinity school worthy of the name required Hebrew as a prerequisite for advanced work. The need for Hebrew instruction was therefore felt. The learned members of the Jewish community could fill this need to a limited extent off campus. Through erudite Protestant clergymen, some additional tu-

---

[1] "Linguistics" and "philology" are often used as though they were synonyms. Linguistics is, strictly speaking, the study of language itself, whereas philology is the critical study of texts. In the present context we mean both: at Penn, Hebrew and the other Semitic languages of the Near East are studied with linguistic as well as philological controls.

telage in Hebrew was also available. But it was inevitable that there was a tension born of the discrepancy between Franklin's guidelines, on the one hand, and the church-oriented faculty and student body, on the other.

All of the University of Pennsylvania provosts were Protestant clergymen until 1868, as were many of the faculty. Though Franklin's founding principles delayed the establishment of a Semitics department at Penn for a century and a half, when it did come, it was dedicated to sound philological, linguistic, and archaeological principles.

To be sure, the pressures of the Age of Enlightenment brought about some temporary, halting steps toward establishing Semitics on the Penn campus. From 1782 to 1784, a scholarly Lutheran clergyman was brought to Penn from Germany: John Christopher Kunze (1744–1807). Germany was the center par excellence for Hebrew and Semitic studies. If any group has pride of place in developing Hebraica into a scientific, academic discipline, it is the intellectual uppercrust of the German, Lutheran clergy. In accordance with this, Kunze came from the ideal circle of Semitic learning. He remained active as a clergyman while he taught at Penn and later at Columbia in New York City. He kept up close contacts with the local scholarly rabbis, who respected his knowledge of Hebrew and sought his opinion on difficult Hebraic questions. His encyclopedic knowledge embraced a mastery of Arabic as well as Hebrew. But Kunze left little but a dim memory behind him on the Penn campus.[2]

As the eighteenth century was drawing to a close, Napoleon invaded Egypt in 1798; this was to be an event of major magnitude in the culture of the Near East and in the intellectual development of the West. Napoleon inaugurated the modern period in the Near East by making Western influence paramount; he started the large-scale study of Egypt and its Pharaonic monuments; and his expedition turned up, in 1799, the Rosetta stone, which proved to be the main key for deciphering the hieroglyphs.[3]

The Rosetta stone is inscribed with the same text in three versions, honoring Ptolemy V Epiphanes in 196 B.C. The first version is Greek, which served as the key to the other two versions, which are Egyptian. The two Egyptian versions are in different scripts: one, in demotic, the other, hieroglyphic. The decipherment was achived by the Frenchman Jean-François Champollion (1790–1832) in 1822 and attracted worldwide attention. In 1858, three University of Pennsylvania undergraduates

[2] In 1828 the Reverend Samuel Brown Wylie was appointed Professor of Classics, when the total University of Pennsylvania faculty numbered only seven persons. His titles varied, and at one time he was called professor of Hebrew, Greek and Latin languages. His role in Hebraica at the University of Pennsylvania was nebulous.

[3] For the decipherments of Egyptian, Babylonian, etc., see my *Forgotten Scripts: Their Ongoing Discovery and Decipherment* (2d ed., New York: Basic Books, 1982).

(Charles R. Hale, S. Huntington Jones, and Henry Morton) published a monograph entitled "Report of the Committee appointed by the Philomathean Society of the University of Pennsylvania to translate the inscription on the Rosetta Stone." The publication is noteworthy in many ways, not the least of which is that it is the first in America on Egyptian philology. It illustrates how intellectual initiative may come from outside the faculty. The nineteenth century was the age of the great decipherments, and Penn was destined to foster the study of the treasures unlocked by the decipherments. But the firstfruits were produced by three undergraduates.

It was during the 1880s that oriental studies took hold at the University of Pennsylvania. We have noted how it could not start with Hebrew, as could other American universities. The inexact, but firmly entrenched, view that Hebrew was sacred, whereas Latin, Greek, and Sanskrit were secular, determined that oriental studies at Penn should start with secular Indo-European studies. And that is what happened.

Morton W. Easton was a disciple of the Yale Sanskritist, William Dwight Whitney (1827–94). Thus, Easton was initiated into the new school of linguistics developed in the wake of Sir William Jones's pioneer observations. But even the Indo-Europeanist Morton Easton was no stranger to Hebrew, for he had in his youth studied for the Baptist ministry. Easton was appointed an instructor in Greek at the University of Pennsylvania in 1884. In addition to his other courses, he taught Sanskrit in 1885–87 to James A. Montgomery and William Romain Newbold, both of the class of '87. James A. Montgomery was to become Penn's leading Hebrew scholar and Semitist for the next half century. William Newbold was to become a professor in the Philosophy Department, but already as an undergraduate, he taught Hebrew to any of his classmates who were interested; Montgomery was among them. Newbold had begun his Hebrew studies at the age of five. He was a brilliant polymath. His publications extended to newly discovered Syriac texts and to Aramaic graffiti in Roman catacombs. In my freshman year (1924–25), I took Newbold's course on "The Development of Christian Thought." His students filled a large lecture hall, and he fascinated us with thrilling tales of contemporary supernatural phenomena, which he (along with other savants at home and abroad in the midtwenties) believed.

Easton was the moving spirit who laid the groundwork for oriental studies at the University of Pennsylvania.[4] At the same time, Morris Jastrow (1861–1921; class of '81) was on the scene. It was Jastrow who

---

[4] For developments from the 1880s to the 1930s, see James A. Montgomery, "Oriental Studies in the University," *The General Magazine and Historical Chronicle* 36 (1933–34) 205–16.

established the first Semitics program that was to endure and grow at Penn.

Until 1876, when the Johns Hopkins University was founded, America had no graduate schools. Germany was the outstanding center of Semitic studies, and it is no accident that by importing the German Semitist, Paul Haupt (1858–1926) in 1883, Johns Hopkins became overnight the leading center for Semitics in America. But Germany retained its prime position in Semitics for a long time to come. It was natural and wise for the young Jastrow to pursue, after graduation in '81, his studies in Holland, France, and especially Germany. His teachers there included some all-time giants in the Semitics field: Theodor Nöldeke, Heinrich Leberecht Fleischer, Franz and Friedrich Delitzsch, Ernest Renan, and the pioneer religionist, Cornelis Petrus Tiele. In addition to learning Semitics, including Assyriology, from the greatest living masters, Jastrow became involved in the new field of comparative religions. This was important for his future service at Penn, where teaching one's own religion was taboo, but where, for that very reason, the objective study of comparative religions was a desideratum. No one can omit religion in a balanced study of virtually any branch of humankind.

Jastrow returned from his studies in Europe in 1885, whereupon he was given a nominal post as Instructor of Semitics. In 1888 he was made assistant librarian in the university library; in 1898, he was promoted to librarian. Meanwhile, in 1891 he was appointed Professor of Semitics which enabled him to establish Penn's first enduring Semitics curriculum.

2. SUDDEN FAME

The man who catapulted the University of Pennsylvania into the forefront of Near Eastern centers on the world scene was Dr. John P. Peters (1852–1921). After studying in Europe, as well as with Whitney at Yale, he was appointed Professor of Hebrew at the Philadelphia Divinity School. In 1886 he was serving as Professor of Hebrew at the University of Pennsylvania. The *Catalogue* for 1887–88 records that he gave the elementary course in Hebrew, which was a junior elective, covering the grammar, translation of Old Testament selections, and composition from English into Hebrew. For 1888–89, Peters announced not only the elementary junior elective, but also the advanced senior elective covering Hebrew syntax, translating selections from the Pentateuch, Psalms, and Prophets, as well as composition and sight-reading.

While Peters was fulfilling his duties as Professor of Hebrew, he became involved in a plan that was much more important, as the future was soon to tell. The plan was to excavate in Babylonia, where European archaeologists (especially the British and French) had unearthed mounds full of texts and monuments. He fixed on Nippur as his site. Such projects require backing. In Provost George Pepper, he had academic support. In Mr. Edward W. Clark he found his Maecenas who underwrote much of the costs and endowed a chair of Assyriology. The expedition was America's first in the Orient; and the chair, America's first endowed position in Assyriology.

With young James Montgomery on hand to teach the Hebrew courses, Peters was free to lead the Babylonian expeditions in 1888–89 and in 1889–90.

A German Assyriologist and Semitist, Dr. Hermann V. Hilprecht (1859–1925), had come to Philadelphia to help out in scholarly matters, specifically concerning discoveries in biblical archaeology, for a journal called the *Sunday School Times*. Peters recognized his talents and made Hilprecht part of the Nippur team. Hilprecht was with Peters in the field on the first campaign in 1888–89.

Nippur yielded many inscribed tablets and other ancient artifacts, which the University of Pennsylvania divided with the Department of Antiquities of the Turkish sultan, for in those days, Mesopotamia was part of the Ottoman Empire. The tablets were important. Nippur was not merely the center of a city-state, but served as a kind of District of Columbia or, better yet, as a sort of Vatican City for the entire Sumero-

Akkadian ecumene. This meant that, in addition to the vast quantities of economic tablets, there were literary, mythological, and religious texts in the temple library. Nippur was the cultic center for the worship of a great cosmic god, Enlil, and his consort, the goddess Ninlil. Much of what we know about Sumerian literature comes from the Nippur excavations, and a handful of dedicated scholars are still (after nearly a century of fruitful labor) piecing together Sumerian literature from the literary fragments from Nippur, divided between Philadelphia and Istanbul. Since Sumerian, which enjoyed enormous prestige and influence throughout the Near East as far back as the Early Bronze Age (3000–2000 B.C.), is the world's first known *lingua franca*, its effects can be felt in the Semitic languages, and, to a lesser extent, in the classical languages of Europe. Penn's discoveries at Nippur keep taking on added meaning as time goes by. Until Peters's expeditions, the University of Pennsylvania was known off campus mainly for its medical and dental schools. But not until the discoveries at Nippur did Penn become famous on the world scene as an intellectual center.

A colleague of Peters, Mr. John H. Haynes (1849–1910), led the third and fourth campaigns at Nippur. The finds kept pouring in, evoking the need for a museum to house and publish them. Thus was born the University Museum, encouraged by Provost Pepper and financially supported by Mr. E. W. Clark. Professor Hilprecht, the first incumbent of the Clark Chair in Assyriology, played a leading role in publishing the Nippur finds, assisted by his staff and students. The Nippur publications of the University Museum have done much to bring the University of Pennsylvania its enduring prestige.

Hilprecht also brought in a galaxy of Assyriologists and archaeologists over the years from Europe. Among them were Stephen Langdon, Arno Poebel (who later formulated a Sumerian grammar in 1923), C. Leonard Woolley (who later headed the epoch-making joint expeditions of the University Museum and British Museum at Ur), and Arthur Ungnad (one of the "greats" in Assyriology and a master of the whole gamut of Semitic languages). The University of Pennsylvania soon became an outstanding training center for young Assyriologist-Semitists under the tutelage of Jastrow and Hilprecht. As the last decade of the nineteenth century dawned, Penn had taken its place among the world's leading centers of Semitic scholarship, a place it still retains.

Franklin's secular principles destined Penn to become a stronghold of objective scholarship, though they delayed the development of Semitic learning by almost 150 years. At the same time, it saved Semitics for a scientific future with strict linguistic-philological and archaeological controls. Paradoxically, it was Hebraists (mainly theologians) who respected and implemented Franklin's secular ideals and embarked on archaeological discovery and philology as the keys to creative scholarship in

Semitics—including Hebrew. Today the only reputable academic approach to the Old Testament is against the background of discoveries from the ancient Near East. Early on, Penn was offering courses on Hebrew not only as a language but also as a vehicle of a Near Eastern culture emerging from the soil. Thus, in the graduate school catalogue of 1906–07, Dr. Albert T. Clay (trained at Penn since 1891 by Jastrow and Hilprecht) offered courses on "Hebrew Archaeology," and on "The Cuneiform Inscriptions and the Old Testament." It is not without interest that the leading handbook on this subject was eventually written by a professor of the University of Pennsylvania, James B. Pritchard, who conceived and edited *Ancient Near Eastern Texts Relating to the Old Testament* (3d ed. with supplement, Princeton: Princeton University Press, 1969), and *The Ancient Near East in Pictures Relating to the Old Testament* (2d ed. with supplement, Princeton: Princeton University Press, 1969). Dr. Pritchard, trained at the University of Pennsylvania,[1] became the curator of the Palestinian section of the University Museum and excavated sites in Palestine and Lebanon.

Semitics at the University of Pennsylvania is a continuous tradition a hundred years old and still going strong.

[1] He took his Ph.D. at Penn in 1942. His thesis, *Palestinian Figurines in Relation to Certain Goddesses Known through Literature. . .* , is published in American Oriental Series 24.

3.   THE JASTROW YEARS

Peters latched onto a vision that he carried out, that of making the University of Pennsylvania famous as a center for Near Eastern studies. Having converted a dream into a reality, Peters left the university in 1893 to return to his theological ambiance. Jastrow's activity at Penn overlapped with Peters'. They were quite different types.

Jastrow was the son of a learned Philadelphia rabbi: Marcus Jastrow, Ph.D., D.Litt., whose *Dictionary of the Targumim, the Talmud Babli and Yerushalmi, and the Midrashic Literature* is based on a staggering body of source material and is so convenient that it is widely used to this day. After graduating from the University of Pennsylvania in the class of '81, Morris Jastrow sat at the feet of the greatest Semitists in Europe. When he returned to America in 1885, he was knowledgeable in Hebrew, Aramaic, Assyriology, Arabic, and other Semitic languages, including Ethiopic, and in the new field of comparative religions. He was appointed to the teaching staff at Penn in 1885 and continued to serve there with distinction until his death in 1921. His period was characterized by intellectual leaders who were polymaths. The number of different subjects he taught at Penn can hardly be approached by academicians today in our age of specialization. While he was teaching, engaging in research and writing, and serving as chairman of one or more departments, he also was responsible for the library of the university. His busy life did not end there; along with Professor Richard Gottheil (1862–1936) of Columbia University, he edited the still useful Semitic Study Series of texts in various Semitic languages. Jastrow was a veritable one-man academy with the inevitable limitation that he could not teach all of his subjects simultaneously. There were not that many hours in the week. To be sure, he had a helpful, though small, supporting staff. In his early years, Hermann V. Hilprecht, whom Peters had brought in, was particularly helpful. And there were others, including James A. Montgomery, destined to lead the department after 1921 when Jastrow passed from the scene. It was characteristic of the period that Jastrow's colleagues did not add to the subjects taught by Jastrow, but they simply made it possible to offer more at any given time than was possible for Jastrow to offer. In those days "there were giants in the land."

The abiding demand within Semitics was for biblical Hebrew, starting at the college level. Thus, among the electives, early on, were elementary Hebrew (open to juniors and seniors) and advanced Hebrew (open to seniors), as noted in the *Catalogue* for 1890–91, for example. Occasionally a third course might be listed, but the two-course offering remained pretty much in place into the thirties. With special permission, of course, a qualified upperclassman could take a more advanced graduate course. The graduate offerings in Hebrew were not limited to the Bible. They might embrace rabbinic texts, inscriptions, and newly discovered literary works, such as the Hebrew original of Ecclesiasticus (otherwise known as The Wisdom of Jesus ben Sirach, or, more briefly, as Ben Sira). But modern Hebrew had not yet become a topic to be taught in colleges and universities.

The pair of undergraduate Hebrew courses were essential but not a challenge for senior faculty. Hence, younger men were hired to give the courses. Montgomery gave them in 1888–90. When Montgomery left to study in Germany for two years (1890–92), Mr. James D. Steele, A.M., LL.B., was appointed Instructor in Hebrew, for 1890–91.

The *Catalogue* for 1892–93 was noteworthy for stating quite plainly that the Hebrew courses are designed for students preparing to enter theology for advanced work and simultaneously as an introduction to postgraduate work in Semitic languages. *Mutatis mutandis*, these two aims remain. The year 1892–93 was noteworthy for the appearance of the talented young Assyriologist and Semitist, Albert T. Clay, on the teaching staff. While Jastrow taught Hebrew 1, and Hilprecht, Hebrew 2, Clay offered advanced Hebrew consisting of a review of the grammar, sight-reading, and composition from English into Hebrew.

In 1893–94, a number of courses taught by Hilprecht, Jastrow, Easton, and others were grouped to constitute the program of History of Religion. This eventually became an independent department in 1910 under the chairmanship of Jastrow, a post he held until he died in 1921.

In 1893–94, the Hebrew courses were reduced from three to two, which apparently met the needs of the undergraduates. Jastrow handled Hebrew 1, while Hilprecht and Clay as a team taught Hebrew 2.

It is sometimes difficult to tell from the catalogues just what was actually offered during some of the years. The catalogues for 1895–96, 1896–97 and 1897–98 no longer list any Hebrew courses among the "free electives." The *Catalogue* for 1901–02 states that Thomas Henry Powers Sailer, Ph.D.,[1] was appointed Instructor of Hebrew, but no courses are listed for him nor even for Professors Hilprecht and Jastrow.

By the time we reach 1906–07, the *Catalogue* contains the curriculum of the graduate school (pages 273–321), and Near Eastern studies is separated into two departments. Since the teaching staff was the same, the need for the division at the University of Pennsylvania may be

---

[1] He received his doctorate at Penn in 1895; his thesis was entitled "Babylonian Contract Tablets."

questioned. On other campuses to this day, a department of archaeology is slanted either toward philology and history or toward anthropology and ethnology. Semitic or classical archaeology cannot be detached from the abundant literature and inscriptions that require the philological/historical approach. American archaeology, as fostered by universities west of the Atlantic Ocean, naturally calls for an anthropological/ethnographic orientation. Methodological pressures needlessly pushed Hilprecht, Jastrow, and Clay into a "schizophrenic" posture, an unnecessary phenomena that could not last. Hilprecht was chairman of Archaeology and Ethnology and taught "Babylonian Palaeography" and "The Interpretation of the Collections of the Babylonian and General Semitic Museum," while Clay taught "Hebrew Archaeology" and gave "Lectures on the Cuneiform Inscriptions and the Old Testament." A holistic approach (and how could scholars like Hilprecht, Jastrow, and Clay avoid it?) required that philological and archaeological materials from the same times and places be correlated. Under the area of Semitic Languages, Jastrow conducted the "Introduction to the Study of Semitic Languages," while Hilprecht and Clay handled Assyriology. It is worth noting that the textbooks used in the courses include Hommel's *Sumerische Lesestücke* and Weissbach's *Die sumerische Frage*. In those days, there were no Sumerologists as distinct from Assyriologists. Every scholar working on Sumerian was conversant with Assyro-Babylonian and with Semitics in general. But not every Assyriologist was capable of engaging in serious Sumerological research. Assyrian and Babylonian are dialects of the well-known Semitic family that embraces Hebrew and Arabic. Sumerian, however, is unrelated to any known family of languages and still poses numerous phonetic, morphological, and lexical difficulties. The fact is that Penn lost no time in entering the Sumerian field, and today the most important undertaking in Near Eastern studies at Penn is the Sumerian Dictionary Project under the directorship of Åke Sjöberg, who holds the Clark Professorship of Assyriology. The tradition of Sumerology at the University of Pennsylvania goes back to the Nippur Expedition in an unbroken chain of tradition established by Peters, Jastrow, and Hilprecht.

Other courses listed in 1906–07 include "Outline of the History of the Ancient Orient," "Lectures on Hebrew Archaeology (Customs and Rites)," "Interpretation of Poetical Books of the Old Testament," "Rabbinic Literature (based on G. Dalman's *Aramäische Lesestücke*)," "Hebrew Fragments of Ecclesiasticus," and "Historical and Archaeological Study of the Pentateuchal Laws." This array of offerings illustrates the impossibility of separating philology from history, the sacred from the profane, or the content of Scripture from history and archaeology.

A course by Clay, "Interpretation of Prophetic Books of the Old

Testament: philological, historical, theological" is noteworthy because of the mention of the "theological" approach (*pace* Franklin!). Greek epic is full of theology, and the Bible is full of profane considerations. There is no hard and fast boundary dividing the secular from the sacred. Our approach should be dictated by the material itself. It is a modern concept that religion and secular life can be hermetically sealed off from each other (as is often meant by the separation of church and state) but in antiquity what we call religion was simply a part of life and no one tried to disentangle them.

Jastrow continued to teach Syro-Aramaic dialects. His course on elementary Aramaic covered the Aramaic parts of the Old Testament (using Strack's *Abriss des Biblisch-Aramäischen*), whereas his Syriac course consisted of the reading of texts in the chrestomathy in Carl Brockelmann's *Syrische Grammatik*. Jastrow at the same time carried full responsibility for a serious Arabic program: "Elements of Arabic Grammar" (based on A. Socin's *Arabische Grammatik*), "Selections from Historical Texts," "Selections from Kalila wa-Dimna" (fables narrated by a pair of jackals in elegant literary Arabic, ultimately based on a Sanskrit original), and "Outline of the History of Arabic Literature." Jastrow also offered "Semitic Epigraphy" consisting of reading Phoenician, Nabatean, and Palmyrene inscriptions.

The *Catalogue* for 1907–08 reflects the continuation of the rich program offered by Hilprecht (chairman), Jastrow, and Clay. The major areas of study consisted of Assyrian, Arabic, Ethiopic, Hebrew, Syriac, and Aramaic. A student minoring in any one of them had to confine his minor courses to that one.

A word should be said about Ethiopic. In the nineteenth century, German scholars made of Ethiopic a discipline by many publications including August Dillman's lexicon and Praetorius's grammar. Actually, Dillman's lexicon (in spite of its lax etymologies) was widely regarded as the best dictionary of any Semitic language through the 1920s. Ethiopia is the African outpost of old Christianity in the Horn of Africa, and is the oldest nation in Africa with a continuous cultural and political history (i.e., till the fall of Haile Selassie). Though the Ethiopic church was independent, it had ties with the Coptic church of Egypt, with which it shares the monophysite doctrine; that is to say, Christ has really only one nature (the divine; his human side is played down). While the University of Pennsylvania has never had on its staff a full-time specialist on Ethiopic (and there are only a few such in the world), Ethiopic has been generally listed among the offerings and was often taught. During the "Montgomery Period," students taking a doctorate in any Semitic language were urged to take one or more courses in every major Semitic language, of which Ethiopic is an important one. I studied Ethiopic for two years with

Montgomery in the late twenties, although there were only two students in the class.[2]

The *Catalogue* of 1907–08 announced courses every year on the grammar and interpretation of various types of literature and the palaeography of the major languages, as well as courses at stated intervals on the life, customs, religion, and history of Semitic nations. In Arabic, Jastrow now added readings from Ibn Khaldun (edited by Macdonald in Semitic Studies Series 4). Ibn Khaldun, from Tunisia, is an important author of the fourteenth century. He is sometimes called the Father of Sociology. Among his observations is the ongoing transition in the Near East from nomadism to village life and urbanism, a process that is now accelerated more than ever. It is curious to observe that during and after World War II, when attention was focused on the Near East, ideas actually fostered by Ibn Khaldun were disseminated as new doctrine in Arab studies. It is worth noting Jastrow's introduction of this author into Penn's Arabic program as an illustration of the University of Pennsylvania's ever expanding horizons. Some repetition in courses is unavoidable; but the introduction of new sources is necessary to keep faculty and students alive intellectually.

Hilprecht also introduced the study of new categories of cuneiform texts. In addition to basic courses on Assyrian grammar and the reading of texts of Delitzsch's chrestomathy, Hilprecht was teaching "Assyrian Historical, and Babylonian Building and Religious Inscriptions" in Rawlinson's *Cuneiform Inscriptions of Western Asia*, volumes 1, 3, 4, and 5, and "Babylonian Letters from Tell el-Amarna." The Amarna Letters are a dossier of about four hundred tablets exchanged between the Pharaohs Amenophis III and IV, on the one hand, and the rulers of western Asia, on the other. They were inscribed from the close of the fifteenth until the middle of the fourteenth century B.C. They are of unique interest as a collection of diplomatic corresondence in antiquity. When the tablets were first found in Egypt in 1887, no one had any inkling that Babylonian was the international written language from Babylonia to Egypt, including Syria-Palestine, Anatolia, and Cyprus. The collection reflects an international order when trade and ideas flowed freely throughout the civilized world, laying the foundation for the emergence of both the Greeks and Hebrews as creative peoples on the stage of recorded history.

[2]In the "good old days," before cost accounting infested our universities, no professor was taken to task by the administration for having only two, or one, or even no students, in a class devoted to a serious academic subject. When I studied Sanskrit with W. Norman Brown at Penn, I was the only student in the class. He was hired and retained for the sake of his subject, Sanskrit, which any serious university requires, whether there are students or not.

The academic year 1909–10 brought a change that was to affect the future of oriental studies at Penn for a quarter of a century. Dr. James A. Montgomery, who was teaching at the nearby Philadelphia Divinity School, was added to the University of Pennsylvania faculty. His courses covered biblical Aramaic, Syriac (the selections read were from the Syriac translation of the Bible called the Peshitta, and the Julian Romance), as well as North Semitic epigraphy. Professor Clay, now the chairman, continued to teach Assyrian and Hebrew. Hilprecht taught Assyrian and Sumerian, while Jastrow offered courses in Hebrew, history of religions, and Arabic. The Arabic readings now included the Ṣaḥīḥ of Al-Bokhari (= traditions of the Prophet Muhammad, which are second only to the Qur'an in authority) and the seven Muᶜallaqat poems (beautiful but difficult pre-Islamic literature). Clay would soon be leaving the University of Pennsylvania for Yale, and Hilprecht for Germany. Jastrow served with distinction until his death in 1921. As events were to show, the continuity of the Pennsylvania tradition of Semitic studies lay on Montgomery's shoulders.

The *Catalogue* of 1910–11 reflects changes. Jastrow, as chairman, had on his staff Assistant Professor Montgomery and two lecturers, the Egyptologist Dr. W. Max Müller and Dr. Benson Brush Charles; Hilprecht and Clay were gone. Ethiopic had been dropped from the roster of courses, but Egyptian was added to the languages in which the graduate student could major. As for Ethiopic, it would continue to reappear. With Egyptian there is a tale of imbalance that requires comment. The two great primary decipherments in the nineteenth century were Egyptian and cuneiform. Both fields are of paramount importance for the history of the Near East and indeed of Western civilization. More specifically, both are components of the world of the Old Testament and, while Akkadian is universally recognized as a Semitic language, Egyptian is also in fact a Semitic (now sometimes called "Hamito-Semitic" or "Egypto-Semitic") language, attenuated through admixtures from Africa and the Mediterranean. Yet only a minority of Semitists reckon with Egyptian, and Old Testament scholars tend to be more cognizant of the cuneiform world than of the Nile Valley. The explanation is not simple, but one factor is inherent in Egypt, Egyptology, and Egyptologists. Unlike ancient Mesopotamia, which was open on all sides and constantly engaged in international give-and-take, Egypt was relatively isolated. Egypt is a long river valley, flanked by mountains and harsh deserts on both sides, and open to the rest of the world only at the northern and southern extremities. Thus, unlike the ever more complex and polyglot culture of the cuneiform world, Egypt developed a distinctive civilization in which the components were harmoniously integrated, so that there was one unified and relatively stable Nile Valley. The ancient Egyptians were happy about their well-watered, fertile valley and regarded themselves as the only first-class human beings. The whole outside world was inhabited by barbarians, and however interesting parts of that world might be as material for diverting tales, it was not fit for civilized Egyptians to live in. Egyptologists tend to become converted (so to speak) into ancient Egyptians psychologically with a relatively isolationist view of the rest of the ancient world. Make no mistake about it: if you have to fall in love with an ancient civilization, you can find no land more seductive than Egypt. Penn could not and did not avoid Egypt. It has sent expeditions into the field, and the University Museum's Egyptian section is one of the finest in America. Moreover the University of Pennsylvania has had an intermittent record of scholarly Egyptological publication and instruction, starting with W. Max Müller in 1910. But while the University has enjoyed an unbroken catena of tradition in Assyriology, Hebrew, and Semitics since the 1880s, this has not been the case with Egyptian.

In 1910–11, Müller started off with a full program in Egyptology, offering elementary Egyptian, hieratic texts for advanced students, elementary Coptic, and Egyptian archaeology. Coptic is the last stage of written Egyptian, employing the Greek alphabet plus a few native signs for sounds not found in Greek. In a sense, one should work back from Coptic, which spells the words with wovels as well as consonants, into the older hieroglyphic Egyptian, which spells consonantally. To use an English example, there are grammatical differences between the present "sing," the past "sang," the past participle "sung," and the noun "song." All (so to speak) would fall together as *sng* in the hieroglyphic writing. Thus, for pronunciation and grammar, we need Coptic, although in an age of specialization, there are some Egyptologists who cannot handle Coptic and Coptologists who cannot read hieroglyphs. Müller, however, had the breadth that characterized his generation.

Jastrow still offered "Introduction to the Study of the Semitic Languages" as well as Hebrew courses on the Pentateuch and on wisdom literature. Together with Charles, Jastrow also offered Arabic courses, which now included selections from the geographical literature (Semitic Studies Series 8) and from the Annals of Tabari (Semitic Studies Series 1).

Montgomery taught an introduction to the Old Testament historical books from Judges forward, a course on Jeremiah, and a seminar on Samuel. His interest and activity continued in Aramaic dialects, with courses on biblical Aramaic, North Semitic epigraphy with special reference to the Aramaic field, and second year Syriac, based on readings from the Julian Romance, Sindban, and the then new Syriac Psalms of Solomon.

The fascicles of the graduate school for 1910–11 have Montgomery offering courses on Ezekiel, and on the religion of the Hebrews, plus a seminar on the latter. Although Montgomery never cut corners on his teaching load, it is doubtful that he could make time simultaneously for all the courses listed in the *Catalogue* plus those in the fascicles of the graduate school. Part of the explanation may lie in the absence of students for some of the esoteric courses.

The graduate school fascicle for 1912–13 has Montgomery offering courses on the postexilic minor Prophets, on the religion of the Hebrews, and on the literature and religion of the Jews from the Greco-Roman Period to the first century A.D. These courses all reflect the growth of a great biblical scholar.

The graduate school fascicle for 1913–14 witnesses an addition to the coverage of Arabic literature offered by Jastrow and Charles: selections from the 1,001 Nights. The Nights are not written in elegant, classical Arabic, nor is the subject matter usually lofty. Arab gentlemen have for centuries read the Nights as escapist literature for personal pleasure, but they often did so as privately as possible so that esteemed friends and family would not find out about it. Yet the Nights are important as a key to popular, male Arab psychology. Arab greatness may be sought in religious, philosophic, and scientific tomes, but the earthy, sensual, and whimsical sides of the traditional Arab are better understood through a reading of the Nights.

That Penn's great Semitists were not oblivious of the less noble frailties of the humanity they studied is also illustrated by a volume published by the University Museum in 1913, to wit, Montgomery's *Aramaic Incantation Texts from Nippur*. That volume is still the authoritative introduction to the whole field of magic bowls from talmudic Babylonia. Now it is universally recognized that the rabbis of Babylonia were part of a culture that fostered not only jurisprudence and folklore, but also reckoned with the occult. Yet for fifty years after the publication of Montgomery's *Incantation Texts*, there were talmudic savants who simply could not get themselves to recognize that there was rabbinic magic in talmudic Babylonia, whose heyday was the Sasanian period (third to seventh century A.D.). For twenty years there was a lull in the study of magic bowls. Then, as a disciple of the master, I undertook the publication of bowl collections in Baghdad, Istanbul, the Louvre, the British Museum, and other repositories at home and abroad, as well as taught courses and conducted doctoral dissertations on the magic bowls. It was characteristic of Montgomery that he never gave courses or conducted dissertations on the subject of a book he had published. In accord with this custom, he never taught me to read bowl texts, but he did suggest, before I sailed in 1931 for a prolonged stay in the Near East, that I look into the Nippur bowls kept by the sultan for his collection in Constantinople (now Istanbul).[3] My emulation of the master, even where specific instruction was absent, tells something of the influence he exerted on me.

[3] I spent September 1931 in Istanbul copying the Nippur bowls for publication. The collection was smaller and in every way inferior to the one in Philadelphia. Being a

In 1914–15, Montgomery was on leave to serve as Director of the American School of Archaeology (later the American School of Oriental Research and now the Albright Institute of Archaeological Research) in Jerusalem. It was an eventful year: the one in which World War I broke out. That Montgomery was accompanied by his wife and three young sons aggravated for him the hazards of war. Palestine then was part of the Ottoman Empire. Although America was not yet involved in the war, it was to be on the side of the (British and French) Allies, while Ottoman Turkey threw in its lot with the (German) Central Powers. Although Montgomery respected the scholarship of Germany and had himself studied there in 1890–92, his sympathies were solidly pro-British, and his church affiliation quite Anglican.

In the fateful year of 1914–15, Jastrow continued as chairman, Dr.'s Müller and Charles stayed on, and Professor Arthur Ungnad joined the staff. Jastrow, Charles, and Ungnad offered a rich variety of courses in Assyriology,[4] including contracts of the Hammurapi and Neo-Babylonian periods (edited by Ungnad in Semitic Studies Series 9, 10), Assyrian historical and building inscriptions, Annals of Assurbanipal, the Abu Habba Cylinder of Nabunaid (edited by Lau in Semitic Studies Series 2, 5), Assyrian and Babylonian letters, and Sumerian business documents. The grammar used was Ungnad's Babylonian-Assyrian grammar, which was superior to anything that preceded it and in its second edition[5] is still excellent and practical, even though much new material is available. Ungnad was one of the most knowledgeable and productive Assyriologists of all time. His command of the tablets was uncanny. Moreover, he was of "the old school" and covered the whole Semitic field. His Syriac and Hebrew grammars are still first-rate and in a class with his Babylonian-Assyrian grammar. He took over Montgomery's area with ease, giving courses on historical books of the Old Testament, biblical Aramaic, and both elementary and advanced Syriac. In those days the outstanding scholars still knew each other's fields. Ungnad's brief stay at the University of Pennsylvania was one of the bright interludes when visiting luminaries added luster to the Pennsylvania tradition.

---

newcomer to the Islamic East, I asked Aziz Bey, the director of the museum in Istanbul, if there were other Nippur bowls in the storage rooms of the museum. He asked what prompted my question, to which I replied it was unthinkable that the sultan gave such a handsome collection to the Americans but kept so little for his own museum. He smiled and said: "You do not yet understand us Turks. When we give, we give the best. Apparently, you Westerners have another concept of generosity."

[4] A preliminary attempt to tell the story of Assyriology in America (including, of course, Penn's prominent role) has been made by C. Wade Meade, *Road to Babylon: Development of U.S. Assyriology* (Leiden: Brill, 1974).

[5] Subsequent, posthumous editions have sacrificed Ungnad's clarity for the sake of additional data.

In 1915–16, Montgomery returned from Palestine to become chairman of the department. Professor Jastrow and Dr.'s Müller and Charles rounded out the department. Jastrow and Charles joined forces in teaching Assyriology. The selections from Sumerian and Babylonian religious texts included litanies, hymns, omens, incantations, and medical tablets. Babylonian and Assyrian creation stories were read. All this, of course, was in addition to the basic and other established offerings.

Jastrow remained active also in the Hebrew program, and among his courses was one on the interpretation of the book of Job. Montgomery taught the introduction to the Old Testament, Jeremiah, advanced Hebrew grammar, biblical Aramaic, first and second year Syriac, and Phoenician and Aramaic inscriptions. Jastrow and Charles teamed up to maintain the Arabic program, adding The Travels of Ibn Baṭṭuṭah (1364–1368/9) to the texts read. Ibn Baṭṭuṭah was a Maghrabi (Far West Arab) from Tangier, Morocco, who set out to see the Muslim world and succeeded in doing so—as far as China! He was able to find employment wherever he went as an Islamic judge (a Qaḍi), for he was a Qur'anic and Islamic scholar well versed in the law. He tells a story well and is not only an important source for geography and events of the fourteenth century, but makes delightful reading. Penn did not make the mistake of staying on dead center. Its Semitists had the wit, interest, and intellectual resources to add constantly to their repertoire. Jastrow maintained this pattern from the beginnings in the 1880s until his death in 1921.

Müller continued to offer elementary Egyptian, religious texts for advanced Egyptian students, elementary Coptic, and an illustrated course on the history of Egypt. Humankind leaves behind not only a written record but also a record of things: monuments great and small. Therefore, history has to be based not only on inscriptions and literature but also on architecture and artifacts. In the case of Egypt, where both the inscriptional and artistic records are so abundant, art and texts have to supplement each other, as Müller well understood. We noted above that Ethiopic might vanish from the scene for a time at Penn, but not for long. No real Semitics program can dispense with it, any more than with Assyrian, Hebrew, or Arabic. Not everyone has a taste for the ecclesiastical literature of Ethiopia. But like it or not, the fact remains that Ethiopic is a key Semitic language with a large literature. It is also a fact that the second largest Semitic-speaking area today is Ethiopia (where the official language is the Semitic Amharic). Arabic is, of course, by far the main Semitic language spoken today. Hebrew, revived in Israel, ranks third, after the Semitic spoken and written in Ethiopia. Müller read selections from the Ethiopic version of the Bible.

For the first time in Penn's history, Turkish was taught (by Charles), with the explanation: "This course in Turkish has been placed here for the sake of convenience." This apologetic note was prompted by one-sided linguistic considerations. Turkish is Ural-Altaic, not Semitic. However, it was written in Arabic script and, since it was developed in the Islamic Ottoman Empire, it is full of Arabic loanwords. Script is often a better indication of culture than language. Wherever the Arabs extended their conquests, they spread, if possible, their language: in Iraq, Syria, Palestine, Egypt, North Africa, and so forth. Where the pre-Islamic language could not be displaced (as in Iran, Turkey, Muslim India, Afghanistan, Indonesia, etc.) it was expressed in Arabic letters. Script, religion, and law are among the potent facts of life that can be more important than the linguistic classification of one's language. Jews have written Arabic, Persian, Greek, German (=Yiddish), Spanish (=Ladino), and so forth in Hebrew letters. Eastern Christianity often uses Greek letters or an offshoot thereof; for example, for writing Coptic. Western Christianity employs the Latin letters. It is script that tells you that Hungarian, Polish, French, and English belong to West European civilization. It is apparent that the apology for listing Turkish in the same department that taught Arabic did not reckon with the fact that the same department was teaching non-Semitic Sumerian because Sumero-Akkadian script links Sumerian and Akkadian inseparably within the same Mesopotamian culture. Sooner or later the Semitists had to come around to one of the most obvious facts of Islam: Arabic, Turkish, and Persian form an inseparable "big three." Much of central Asia has reckoned with Turkish as the language of home and marketplace, but with Persian as the medium of belles lettres, and with Arabic as the language of religion and law. (The twentieth century has witnessed the inroads of Russian and Chinese, but the background remains the same.) Now, especially since World War II, there is nothing odd about Semitic Arabic, Indo-European Persian and Ural-Altaic Turkish being taught in the same Islamic (or oriental, or Near Eastern, or even Semitics) department, at Penn or anywhere else.

We should also observe that Assistant Professor Roland G. Kent (1877–1952) was now (1915–16) offering Old Persian based on Tolman's *Ancient Persian lexicon and Texts,* a hardy perennial still used when I studied Old Persian with Kent in the late twenties. The Old Persian texts are the cuneiform lapidary inscriptions of the Achaemenian kings: Cyrus, Darius, Xerxes, Artaxerxes, and so forth from the sixth to fourth century B.C. The four royal names just mentioned are all in the Bible.[6] Old Persian is therefore a source of prime importance for the last major period in Old Testament history. Furthermore, most of the Old Persian

---

[6] Normative Jewish tradition, following the Bible, reckons only with these four names, as though there had been only one king bearing each name. King Cambyses, son of Cryus the Great, marched through Palestine to conquer Egypt in 525 B.C. Although he is mentioned in the Aramaic papyri by the Jews of Elephantine, he is completely overlooked in rabbinic literature as well as in the Bible.

texts are trilingual: Old Persian, Elamite, and Babylonian. It was the decipherment of Old Persian that opened up the whole field of Assyriology, ultimately including Sumerian. Montgomery advised me to study Persian because of its bearing on the Semitic field—good advice, which I followed. Quite close to Old Persian is the Zoroastrian Avesta; Kent taught both elementary Avestan, and the old Gathas of the Avesta. Persian is important for studies pertaining to the Semites throughout the Babylonian, Syro–Aramaic (including talmudic) and Islamic periods. In our age of specialization, not every Semitist knows Persian, but no real university can afford to disregard it.

The graduate school announcement for 1916–17 records that Jastrow resumed his chairmanship, while his staff consisted of Professor Montgomery, Professor Müller, and Dr. Chiera. (Charles had left the scene.) Edward Chiera (1885–1933) was one of the most gifted copyists in the annals of Assyriology. Most of us copy one sign at a time. Chiera had an eagle-eye and a remarkable span of vision. He would look at a whole line, shift his eyes from the tablet to the sheet of paper, and dash off the whole line legibly and beautifully. He was for the most part accurate, but such genius may lapse into little errors that plodding and less gifted scholars usually avoid. Trained by Jastrow, Chiera was the link that kept the Assyriological tradition alive at Penn without a break. In calling Chiera a copyist, we must avoid the implication that he merely transcribed the three-dimensional signs on tablets into their two-dimensional equivalents on paper. He had a feeling for the people and life recorded in the tablets. He eventually wrote a book called *They Wrote on Clay*,[7] a charming as well as authoritative (but popular) book that reckons with the men and women for whom the tablets were written and with their worldly concerns. With Chiera's advent there appears a new course, "Practical Exercises in Copying Tablets."

Jastrow kept active in teaching both Assyrian and Hebrew. Montgomery taught Old Testament archaeology and a couple of biblical texts (Isaiah, chaps. 1–35, and a selection of Psalms). He also taught the Elephantine papyri (Aramaic documents of the Jewish commercial and military colony functioning in the fifth century B.C. in the service of the Persian Empire that then included Egypt). Elephantine is an island in the Nile at Aswan. The role of the colony was the supervision of trade and other relations between Egypt and Nubia. Many commodities, notably gold and ivory, were imported into Egypt, the Near East, and the Aegean from Black Africa via Elephantine. The Jews had a temple there, where they offered sacrifices to their ancestral god whom they called

---

[7] Edward Chiera died in Chicago in 1933 from bone cancer. His book, which appeared posthumously, is entitled *They Wrote on Clay: The Babylonian Tablets Speak Today* (Chicago: University of Chicago Press, 1938). The University of Chicago Press later issued it in paperback.

Yahu (= Yahweh). They knew no Hebrew but they called themselves either the Jews (actually, Judeans), or the Arameans, of Yeb (= Elephantine). They had no Hebrew writings, biblical or otherwise. Their origin is still disputed,[8] but that they were Yahwistic Jews is certain. Elephantine opened new historic horizons, and it is characteristic of Penn in general and of Montgomery in particular that horizons kept expanding with the new discoveries.

Among the new courses offered by Montgomery, Mandaic now made its appearance. The all-time exemplary Semitist, the German Theodor Nöldeke, published in 1875 his *Mandäische Grammatik*. For more than half a century it was widely considered the finest grammar of any Semitic language. Other European scholars also immersed themselves in the Mandeans and their literature. The Mandeans are a small sect of Gnostics in southern Iraq and adjacent parts of Iran whose priests have preserved a knowledge of the sect's ancient scriptures. The major Mandean documents were published by Mark Lidzbarski. One of them, The Ginza Rabba (The Great Treasure), was read in Montgomery's Mandaic class in 1916–17. Mandaic studies waned thereafter but eventually experienced a renaissance.[9] They are important for a number of fields. The Aramaic

[8] In the tenth century B.C., King Solomon not only (re)conquered Syrian districts but established colonies of Israelites there (2 Chr 8:1–6). After his death, his realm fell apart with the division of the homeland into the southern kingdom of Judah and the northern kingdom of Israel. Obviously, most of the foreign empire—such as Syria—was lost. His colonies were to maintain security and facilitate trade for their sovereign. Under new masters, they were available to serve as experienced commercial and military colonies. Cut off from their homeland, they gradually forgot Hebrew and spoke Aramaic—the language of Syria. In Solomon's days, there was no canonical Bible and no literary prophetic movement, nor any established centrality of cult. The Elephantine colony corresponded with both Jerusalem and Samaria (Mt. Gerizim). Multiple temples such as those at Jerusalem, Mt. Gerizim, and Elephantine were the norm. The colony knew that they were Yahwistic Judeans, for in Solomon's reign the tribe of the king was Judah and allegiance to Yahweh was a fait accompli. We know from the Elephantine papyri that the Jews were already established on Elephantine before Cambyses conquered Egypt in 525 B.C. It is possible that the Assyrian conquerors of Egypt (Esarhaddon and Assurbanipal) imported the Judean colony from Syria to manage and defend the gateway to inner Africa because foreign mercenaries are more reliable than native sons, who understandably would be prone to rebel against the invaders of their country.

[9] The late Lady E. Stefana Drower is the principal architect of the revival in Mandaic studies. She was in Baghdad as the wife of Sir Edwin Drower, a British judge there during the thirties and forties, and she felt a need to accomplish something intellectually significant. Being another social butterfly in the foreign colony in Baghdad was not enough for her. She consulted Moses Gaster, the authority on the Samaritans, in London. He told her that the Samaritans were the most fascinating people in the world, but that the Mandeans were the second best. He oriented her in regard to cultivating the friendship and trust of the Mandean priests and learning their language. She succeeded admirably. Though not a trained Semitist, she immersed herself in Mandaean language, custom and lore. Unlike Nöldeke, she reckoned not only with the classical but also with the postclassical Mandaic texts and the current language cultivated by the priests. She had

dialects of the Babylonian Talmud are closely related to Mandaic, and it is realistic to say that Mandaic is about the best linguistic aid one can have for tackling the problems of talmudic Aramaic. Soon after World War II, Gnostic papyri found near Nag Hammadi in Egypt, though in Coptic, turned out in part to be translations of Mandaic originals. If students took advantage of Montgomery's offerings, they could get a head start in their careers as productive scholars in ancient Near Eastern studies.

Montgomery and Jastrow joined forces in the Arabic program. In addition to some classics that were new to the Penn curriculum, selections from the Qur'an were also read.

I studied Qur'an a decade later with Montgomery. Montgomery loved Arabic but disliked Muhammad, whom he considered an imposter. However, even though religious conviction got in the way of Montgomery's evaluation of Muhammad as a Prophet, he never lost sight of the fact that the Qur'an must remain the cornerstone of Arabic studies. Classical Arabic is Qur'anic, and Montgomery told me that as a young scholar he had read the Qur'an from cover to cover, and he counseled me to do the same, because no one who had not done so could become a serious Arabist.

Müller, now an Assistant Professor, offered, in addition to the program in Egyptology, modern Arabic for the first time at the University of Pennsylvania. The course was based on the dialects of Egypt. This was long before modern Arabic had become a subject that universities would condescend to handle. The Penn faculty were not only savants deeply rooted in classical learning and in the past; they were pioneers who blazed future trails.

Also, for the first time, second year Ethiopic was taught (by Müller). It happens that the Ethiopic Bible contains apocryphal and pseudepigraphical books, which are often lost in the Hebrew originals and in other translations, including the Greek, from which the Ethiopic was often made. The best record of pseudepigraphic books such as Jubilees and Enoch is in Ethiopic. Müller announced he would read apocalyptic books (of which there is a plethora in Ethiopic) with his students. A decade later, I read such Ethiopic scriptures with Montgomery for two years, following the path blazed by Müller.

While he was teaching courses in Egyptology, Arabic, and Ethiopic, Müller also offered North Semitic epigraphy. Doubtless such versatility

---

already learned to speak the vernacular Arabic of Iraq. Her first book on the subject (*The Mandaeans of Iraq and Iran: Their Cults, Customs, Magic, Legends and Folklore* [Oxford: Clarendon Press, 1937]) is useful, very interesting, but immature compared with the mastery she eventually achieved. She acquired a large number of sacred texts and published quite a few of them. Having begun her Mandaic studies when she was already middle-aged, she luckily had a long life, and when she died in her eighties, E. Stefana Drower was the world's leading figure in Mandaica.

precludes being a meticulous specialist in each of the many fields that Müller knew, but it makes possible the creation of remarkable books such as Müller's *Asien und Europa nach altaegyptischen Denkmälern (Asia and Europe according to Old Egyptian Monuments)*, 1893. We are moving into an era where high specialization is indispensable, but this need not prevent us from appreciating individuals of a now extinct species, like Alexander von Humboldt.

In the academic year 1917–18 Montgomery was chairman, supported by a staff consisting of Professor Jastrow, Assistant Professors Müller and Husik, and Dr. Chiera. Something should be said about the new face: Isaac Husik. Husik was a versatile linguist. He knew Latin, Greek, Hebrew, Aramaic, and Arabic, plus the usual modern languages. He knew the rabbinic field well. He was a graduate jurist (though he did not elect to practice law). His field was philosophy. He handled ancient Greek philosophy masterfully. His book *History of Medieval Jewish Philosophy* (1916) is still widely read and often considered authoritative. His hold on medieval philosophy was thorough, whether dealing with the Muslim Averroes, the Jewish Maimonides, or the Christian Thomas Aquinas. His attractive volumes in the Schiff series of Jewish classics on the Book of Principles by Joseph Albo (with the English translation and Hebrew original on opposing pages) is standard. Husik lacked charisma; no one ever considered him a good lecturer. But he could do what the glamorous professors of philosophy or classics could not do. He could lead the qualified student through a great text, phrase by phrase, sentence by sentence, and paragraph by paragraph, so that the student was brought into contact with a great thinker of the past. I read Aristotle's *Peri Psyches* (in Latin called the *De Anima*) with Husik, and the magic of Husik was not that he charmed anyone but that he brought us face to face with Aristotle, without intruding himself. So though Husik was not original or creative, he familiarized me with Aristotle who is greater than any professor we are likely to meet in our life times. Husik had in his youth wanted to become a rabbi. But he also studied philosophy and science and was torn between faith and reason. The old solution to the dilemma that prevailed from Philo Judaeus (first century B.C. and first century A.D.) until Spinoza (seventeenth century A.D.) was through allegorical interpretation, whereby Jewish revelation could be harmonized with Greek philosophy. In the Middle Ages, Muslim, Jewish, and Christian philosophers agreed that Aristotle was the philosopher par excellence whose truth squared with Scripture once the latter was interpreted allegorically. Spinoza finally divorced reason from revelation. In his formative years, Husik agonized over the conflict and abandoned his plan to become a rabbi, but he never gave up his love of tradition and study. It was a great experience to read Averroes, Maimonides, or St. Thomas with Husik, who was living through the problem with which those giants of the Middle Ages grappled. Usually Jewish scholars deal with Maimonides's *Guide of the Perplexed* in Hebrew translation—but not Husik. We studied the *Guide* in the Arabic original in order to follow the very words of the dean of Jewish philosophers. The classes were small but choice. It was a privilege not only to sit at the feet of the teacher but also to be with fellow students who could study philosophical texts in Latin, Greek, Hebrew, or Arabic. After Husik, my other professors of philosophy seemed somewhat amateurish.

Husik's lecture course was entitled "History of Jewish Philosophy, Lectures and Papers, Judeo-Alexandrian School, the Medieval Aristotelians and Neo-Platonists from Saadia to Joseph Albo."

Jastrow and Chiera shared the teaching of Assyriology, strengthening the link in the Pennsylvania tradition. Jastrow also offered a "Public Course" where a biblical book was read in English translation with explanatory comments by the professor. The readings selected for 1917–18 were the prophecies of Isaiah. Jastrow felt the importance of what we now call "out reach" because ultimately we depend on the public for support. A public that understands and enjoys the fruits of scholarship is more likely to support it.

Montgomery continued to teach Old Testament religion and the interpretation of biblical books plus Ben Sira, Syro-Aramaic dialects, and northwest Semitic inscriptions.

Jastrow and Montgomery both taught classical Arabic while Müller again offered the modern Arabic of Egypt. In addition to his offerings in ancient Egyptian, Müller deepened his program in Ethiopic studies by offering a third year course based on the reading of pseudepigraphical books. As far as I know, this marked the all-time apex of Ethiopic studies at Penn.

Much the same program was offered in 1918–19 as in the preceding year. However, Jastrow, Montgomery, and Müller all offered courses in classical Arabic, listing some authors for the first time at Penn: thus, The Travels of Ibn Jubair, The Story of Antar, Yakut's Geograpical Dictionary and Abdul-Feda's *Historia Anteislamica*.

Majors in 1919–20 included Assyrian, Arabic, Egyptology, Hebrew, and Aramaic Dialects. Ethiopic had again vanished, for Müller had gone. The most noteworthy changes were the new Arabic readings offered by Jastrow and Montgomery, namely, selections from Ibn Hisham's Life of Muhammad, from Shahrastani's Book of Religious and Philosophical Sects, and from Buladhuri's work, The Conquest of Islam.

The academic year 1920–21 witnessed a new appointment: Assistant Professor Frederick Lutz to fill the void left by Müller in Egyptology. Jastrow was chairman, with Professor Montgomery, Assistant Professors Husik and Lutz, and Dr. Chiera to share the teaching load.

Montgomery offered the book of Daniel, anticipating his distinguished commentary, *Daniel,* that appeared in 1927 in the International Critical Commentary series. His other course covered biblical Aramaic and Targums (Aramaic versions of biblical books).

Lutz gave three Egyptian courses: elementary Egyptian, based on Erman's Egyptian grammar and chrestomathy, religious texts for advanced students, and Coptic, based on Steindorff's *Koptische Grammatik* and chrestomathy.

In 1921, during his leave for 1921–22, Jastrow died. His passing marked the end of an era. He had been on the faculty from the beginnings in the 1880s. He was an integral part of the departmental programs in Hebrew, Arabic, Assyriology, and history of religions. That he made time for so much teaching, research, and publication in so many areas, in addition to serving as librarian of the university, tells much but not all of the story. John Peters' accomplishment was stellar and brief, like the passing of a brilliant meteor. Jastrow's achievement, though less flashy, required hard and relentless work for the span of a long generation.

The Jastrow years were darkened by an open rift known as the Peters-Hilprecht Controversy. Dr. Peters was not a professional archaeologist nor a trained Assyriologist. He happened to be one of several American Near Eastern academicians who constituted an informal committee to plan a U.S. archaeological expedition in Mesopotamia. Sometimes a person's achievement is greater than that person. Such was Peters' launching of the Nippur expedition. Inspired by the dream of America's future role in unearthing the cities of Mesopotamia and their archives, he seized the initiative that catapulted America into the select company of nations exacavating in Mesopotamia and the University of Pennsylvania into the category of world-famous universities. But whereas Peters' vision, planning, initiative, and labor sufficed to launch the Nippur expedition, they were not enough to sustain the operation during the years and decades ahead. Peters at first embraced the collaboration of Dr. Hermann Hilprecht, who came to America primarily to cover biblical archaeological news for the *Sunday School Times.* The dual role—and dual nature—of Hilprecht explains some of the friction and notoriety that eventually surfaced as a cause célèbre that is not yet forgotten.

Hilprecht was an able Semitist, cuneiformist, and archaeologist, but at the same time, he was a journalist. The exactness expected of professional scholars does not mix with a journalist's need to interest the lay reader without too much concern for the details. The standards of "truth" are not identical in the two professions of scholarship and journalism.

Peters could not help realizing that he was unqualified to stay on top of the Nippur project, and that his assistant, Hermann Hilprecht, was much better qualified. Peters soon pulled out of the University of Pennsylvania and out of the Nippur expeditions to take a post in Old Testament at a theological school in New York City, for which he was better trained. But seeing Hilprecht inheriting the empire that he (Peters) had fashioned, was too much for Peters to bear in silence.

Peters contrived a case against Hilprecht. Tablets had been found in Nippur, though few had been made available. Hilprecht had an Assyriologist's estimate of the situation; the rest of the world, including Peters, did not. But, Hilprecht—journalist that he was—did not hesitate to use as illustrations tablets from other sites that were acquired by purchase, giving the impression that they were from Nippur. In the halls of academe, Hilprecht was guilty of a mortal sin; among journalists he had barely committed a peccadillo. Why should a journalist worry about the source of a tablet used to illustrate cuneiform writing? "If you've seen one, you've seen them all," (as Spiro Agnew once said of slums). Or, as a New Yorker might say: "Nippur, shmippur! Just so long as you're healthy."

On the next point, my sympathies are all with Hilprecht. He hailed the Nippur tablets as embracing a great "library." His critics, headed by Peters, accused him of gross distortion. How right Hilprecht was is now obvious. The literary tablets from Nippur are the cornerstone of recovering the great Sumerian poetic tradition: the world's earliest known real literature. Hilprecht knew this from his first hand familiarity with the tablets. Peters and others pounced on the few "illustrative" tablets as the basis for branding Hilprecht's claims as false and for discrediting him as a scholar in the newspapers as well as in academic circles.

Other accusations were leveled at Hilprecht, but our moral judgment should be tempered with an awareness of the times. Those were the days when Mesopotamia was part of the Ottoman Empire, and everything found by the excavators belonged to the Sublime Porte. The latter, as absolute monarch, could give any of the Nippur antiquities to whom he pleased. In accordance with the traditions of Near Eastern generosity, the sultan presented some of the finds to Hilprecht. Hilprecht had the right to accept them, though he would have avoided censure if he had quietly donated all (and not merely some of) them to the Nippur collection in the museum of the University of Pennsylvania.

I know that some of the Nippur finds are in the Frau Professor Hilprecht Collection of Babylonian Antiquities at the University of Jena. The late Professor Julius Lewy gave me photographs of magic bowls from Nippur, which are in the Hilprecht collection at Jena, and which I subsequently published. It would be more charitable to speak of Hilprecht's behavior as unwise, rather than wrong.

Peters' going public with his accusations impelled Hilprecht to demand that the University of Pennsylvania conduct a trial so that he could defend himself and be vindicated. He did just that and wrote up the trial, presenting the testimony, pro and con, with many sundry aspects of the proceedings, and his official vindication.[10] He was found "not guilty" on all scores. Had Hilprecht not requested the trial, he would have come off better. (When we are falsely accused, silence may be wiser than demanding a trial which is sure to broadcast the accusations to a still wider public.) It was the trial that made the controversy more notorious than ever.

Hilprecht was unpopular and often tactless with his colleagues. One of my teachers, George A. Barton, who was involved in the case, had a low opinion of Hilprecht's standards of veracity. In the summer of 1931, I was a member of the expedition of Beth-Zur along with Dr. Clarence Fisher, who had served as an architect under Hilprecht at Nippur. I must warn the reader that Fisher, though a masterful field-archaeologist, was something of a gossip. When Sir Flinders Petrie came out with his gossipy autobiography called *Seventy Years in Archaeology*, Fisher told me he would like to write a counterpart entitled *Digging Up Their Pasts*. In any event, Fisher informed me that Hilprecht kept his office at the University Museum locked, and that in a specific locked drawer of his desk in that office he declared he had the excavated evidence to prove his claims. Fisher broke into the office through the transom, jimmied open the drawer, and found in it absolutely nothing. As soon as the break-in became known, Hilprecht hastily boarded a trans-Atlantic liner bound for Europe. This is what Fisher told me. Whatever it may lack in truth, it makes up in sensationalism. Scholars may rightly scorn it, whereas journalists may welcome it with open arms.

Most of the testimony at the trial was hostile to Hilprecht. One witness however, Dr. Hugo Radau, had nothing but unmingled praise for his teacher, Hermann Hilprecht. As a witness testifying at Hilprecht's trial, Radau pointed out something that many historians of antiquity have yet to learn, to wit, that centers like Nippur were university cities. It is a pity that an able scholar like Radau, with such breadth of vision as well as detailed knowledge, dropped out of international scholarship after a most promising start. It was not until I became immersed in Ebla studies that I fully realized that already in the Early Bronze Age, cuneiform centers with archives and libraries constituted not only intellectual centers, where scribes were trained in all the arts and sciences of their day, but also formed part of a university system, with student and faculty exchange. The "universities" even used the same textbooks as their sister universities hundreds of miles away. We cannot view the Early Bronze Age in the Near East as prehistoric, let alone primitive.

[10] See Hilprecht's *The So-called Peters-Hilprecht Controversy*, Part I: *Proceedings of the Committee Appointed by the Board of Trustees of the University of Pennsylvania to Act as a Court of Inquiry;* Part II: *Supplemental Documents, Evidence and Statement* (Philadelphia: A. J. Holman & Co., 1908).

Though Hilprecht won the case, his Pyrrhic victory was soon followed (in 1910) by the end of his academic career, and the very mention of his name is more likely to conjure up recollections of the controversy than of his important contributions to learning and to the Pennsylvania tradition.

Though Peters left Penn in 1893, his resentment took over a decade to incubate. The controversy raged from 1905 to 1908. Hilprecht detested Jastrow's testimony against him even more than Peters' accusations. For Hilprecht felt that Peters at least came out in the open as an accuser, whereas Jastrow "refused" to "accuse" his colleague but agreed only to "testify against" him. A subtle distinction that Hilprecht, understandbly enough, failed to appreciate. Thus, relations within the department were not all sweetness and light, despite the great creativity that we can appreciate in retrospect.

4. THE MONTGOMERY YEARS

Jastrow's death in 1921 stripped Penn of a versatile and productive Semitist, but it did not break the tradition in any of Jastrow's fields. Chiera was there to carry on in Assyriology and Montgomery in all the other branches of Semitics. Moreover, Montgomery was to remain active on the campus for over a quarter of a century and assume the headship of the department for over twenty years.

Aside from the serious loss of Jastrow, 1921–22 saw the same faculty as the previous year: Montgomery (chairman), Husik, Chiera, and Lutz. Two courses on archaeology were offered: on Palestine, by Montgomery; and on Egypt, by Lutz. Lutz taught Egyptian texts of the Greco-Roman period (Rosetta stone, decree of Canopus, the bilingual decrees of Philae, and the stela of Alexander II), as well as the translation of hieratic texts in Möller's *Hieratische Lesestücke*.

A hiatus in the Egyptian program occurred in 1922–23, for Lutz had left. The staff was now limited to Professor Montgomery (the chairman), Professor Husik, and Assistant Professor Chiera. Chiera carried the entire Assyrian program including Babylonian parallels to the Old Testament. In a crisis year, after the death of Jastrow and the departure of Lutz, Chiera put his shoulder to the wheel and helped out in yeomanlike fashion with the entire Semitics program. He gave the Hebrew course on the book of Isaiah and teamed up with Montgomery to cover "Arabic and Ethiopic." Having been trained in the University of Pennsylvania tradition, Chiera[1] could take on the teaching of Hebrew,[2] Arabic, and Ethiopic, but his heart was in cuneiform, and the other topics he took on dutifully rather than joyously. However, he understood the value of those other subjects, and it was his advice that turned Solomon Skoss (later Professor of Arabic at Dropsie College) into an Arabist. Noteworthy is the very fact that Ethiopic, which had lain dormant, was resurrected, and selections from Ghazali were introduced into the repertoire of Arabic texts studied in class.

Montgomery's new course was "Judaistic Literature: Apocrypha,

[1] Edward Chiera's doctoral thesis (1913) is embodied in his *Legal and Administrative Documents from Nippur Chiefly from the Dynasties of Isin and Larsa* (Philadelphia: University Museum, 1914).

[2] Though he was Italian, Chiera was a Protestant clergyman, with the degrees of Bachelor of Divinity (1911) and Master of Theology (1912) from Crozer Theological Seminary. He was therefore no stranger to Hebraic studies.

Pseudepigrapha, etc.: introduction, religious contents." Egyptology had been put on the backburner, for no one was there to teach it and all the *Catalogue* remarked about Egyptian was "Courses to be announced." Although Egyptology is a must for oriental studies at Penn, it has (unlike Assyriology) passed through periods of suspended animation.

In 1923–24 there was a new face. Professor George A. Barton (1859–1942) left Bryn Mawr College to take over the chairmanship of the department at Penn, now called Semitic Languages and Archaeology. His staff consisted of Professors Montgomery and Husik and Assistant Professor Chiera. Barton covered more fields than any of my teachers at the University of Pennsylvania. He taught the whole range of Egyptology, Assyriology, Old and New Testament, history of religions, archaeology and so forth and published voluminously. His commentary on Ecclesiastes in the International Critical Commentary series gave him a place in Old Testament studies. To say that he worked in the whole field of Assyriology does not convey an adequate impression of his scope. He published tomes on Sumerian, Assyrian, Babylonian epigraphy, and more, and even taught and wrote on a new, pioneering cuneiform field: Hittite. He was dauntless. He leaped into the Egyptological breach with courses on elementary Egyptian, Pyramid Texts and the Book of the Dead for advanced students, elementary Coptic, and Egyptian archaeology. His course on comparative Semitic grammar embraced comparisons with the Hamitic languages: a comparative field still fraught with pitfalls. Barton offered a pair of courses on Old Testament books. And with Chiera he assumed responsibility for a large array of Akkadian and Sumerian courses and one on Mesopotamian archaeology. He was concurrently Professor of New Testament at the Philadelphia Divinity School on which campus he lived. He was a "one-man oriental institute," though he was not attuned to the stricter disciplines such as linguistic science.

Montgomery offered a course on the philological study of the later books of the Hebrew canon, while the Arabic and Ethiopic program was handled jointly by Barton, Montgomery, and Chiera. In addition, Chiera conducted a course on the comparative study of Pentateuchal and Babylonian laws.

There were no faculty changes in 1924–25. Montgomery's course on the pagan religions of Syria and Arabia required the ability to read "Semitic, Greek and Latin texts." This prerequisite sums up the standards maintained by Montgomery. Cuneiform Hittite, taught by Barton, was an innovation in the University of Pennsylvania program in 1924–25.

In the autumn of 1924, I entered Penn as a freshman. The undergraduate offerings tended to be limited to an elementary and an intermediate course in biblical Hebrew. Davidson's rather jejune and pedestrian *Hebrew Grammar* was used. Montgomery and Chiera were often pressed into service for these basic courses. If undergraduates were good enough, they would be permitted to enter graduate courses with the permission of the instructor. I majored in Hebrew and was given advanced credit for the basic Hebrew courses because of extracurricular training in Hebrew. During my college years (1924–27), I was graduated in Hebrew studies from Gratz College (class of '26) and I also took all of Professor Margolis's courses in biblical philology at Dropsie College for four consecutive years. Solomon Skoss's courses at Dropsie in classical and Judeo-Arabic were of great use to me, too. I also studied Talmud under Solomon Zeitlin at Dropsie. The presence and quality of Dropsie relieved Penn from the burden of teaching rabbinic literature in those days. But from my undergraduate days, Professor Montgomery was my major professor and supervisor, and I regard him as my academic father.

The following year (1925–26) saw Montgomery back in the chairmanship, where he was to remain for a decade. Professors Barton and Husik and Assistant Professor Chiera also stayed on. The new instructor was Dr. Ephraim A. Speiser (1902–1965), who had been trained in Semitics and in biblical philology by Margolis at Dropsie College, where he took his Ph.D. Speiser was studying Assyriology with Chiera. The two became interested in the Nuzi tablets and worked together on them. Those cuneiform texts were excavated from the middle twenties to the early thirties at the mound of Nuzi near the modern city of Kirkuk, in northeastern Iraq. They were written over a period of four or five generations in the Amarna age (fifteenth and fourteenth centuries B.C.) and provide a more intimate picture of family life and urban sociology than any other archives from remote antiquity. Real estate transactions, marriages, divorces, wills, adoptions, lawsuits, and so forth give us close views of personal and family life during a period that is documented more fully (throughout the Near East from Egypt to Mesopotamia) than many subsequent historic eras. One of the most interesting dossiers from Nuzi is the damaging testimony of the citizens of Nuzi against their corrupt mayor, Kushiharpe, who was implicated in ail sorts of malfeasance, misfeasance, and moral turpitude. While the language of the tablets is Babylonian, the names of the people (as well as many loanwords and "barbarisms" in the local Babylonian dialect) showed that the population and native speech were Hurrian. Hurrian happens to be a major factor in the history of the entire Near East, especially throughout the second millennium B.C. Chiera and Speiser collaborated on the Nuzi tablets and the Hurrian problem. After 1928, when Chiera left the University of Pennsylvania to join the Oriental Institute of the University of Chicago, it was Speiser who developed the Pennsylvania tradition of Assyriology, and (among other aspects of cuneiform studies) perpetuated the interpretation and publication of the Nuzi tablets. I was one of his students and, in the half-century that followed, I saw to it that Nuzi studies were developed and transmitted to new generations of students wherever I taught, whether at Johns Hopkins, Dropsie, Brandeis, or New York University.

Assyriology was now shared by Barton, Chiera, and Speiser without significant changes in the course offerings.

The announcement for 1926–27 reflects no change in faculty. Montgomery was in sole charge of the Arabic and Ethiopic program which now included a seminar on the South Arabic inscriptions. Unless one has seen Montgomery's files on South Arabic, it would be hard to realize how deeply he had gone into this esoteric fringe of the Semitic world.[3] Montgomery felt that scholars should control the main aspects of their respective fields, but should also work on one or more of the less frequented byways. It is the latter that often provides the ingredient that sparks creativity.

Montgomery also offered general Semitics courses, to wit, "Religion of the Hebrews," "Judaistic Literature before the New Testament" (in the original languages), and "Rabbinic Literature" (Targums, Mishna, etc.). Montgomery was broad enough, but he did not overextend himself. He scrupulously avoided the vast fields of Assyriology and Egyptology. His grasp of comparative Semitic grammar was masterful, and for this he controlled Akkadian grammar; but he kept away from the cuneiform texts. I do not recall that he ever referred to the Egyptian language in class. His common sense required that he avoid the bottomless pit of Egypto-Semitics. Egyptian history was another matter. He needed it for his biblical studies—especially for his commentary on Kings in the International Critical Commentary series, which was his last book, published posthumously. To be the author of two great commentaries in this prestigious series tells something about the man.

Barton was now in charge of oriental archaeology, on which he offered three courses: Mesopotamian archaeology, Egyptian archaeology, and Palestinian archaeology. It was humanly impossible for Barton to do justice to all the fields for which he assumed responsibility. One of the casualties was Egyptology, now reduced to his one course, "Elements of the Grammar and Interpretation of Selected Texts."

In 1927–28, Speiser was away on leave for field work in Iraq. He decided to excavate at two sites in the Mosul area. One of them was Tepe Gawra, a steep mound of about twenty strata, the last of which terminated in a single tower datable to around the middle of the second millennium B.C. Tepe Gawra proved to be an important, well-stratified connecting link from Neolithic times in the fifth millennium to the midsecond millennium B.C. The other mound, Tell Billa was not so

---

[3] One of Montgomery's last students, Dorothy Stehle, wrote her thesis on South Arabic, namely, *Sibilants and Emphatics in South Arabic* (University of Pennsylvania, published in *Journal of the American Oriental Society*, 60 [1941]).

unusual. It was the ancient Shibaniba, after which a gate at Nineveh was named. It did produce Hurrian pottery and some cuneiform tablets,[4] and Speiser had hoped, though in vain, that it would be an important Hurrian capital. But the two mounds were sufficiently close to be excavated by the same expedition, housed in one and the same local village. I was on the field staff that excavated Tell Billa and Tepe Gawra in 1931–32, when Speiser was director, and in 1932–33 and 1934–35, when Charles Bache directed it. This was done as a joint expedition of the University Museum and the American School of Oriental Research in Baghdad. The interplay between the campus department, the University Museum, and the archaeological work in the field was close and reflects the scope of what was then called the Department of Semitic Languages and Archaeology.

My first year as a graduate student was 1927–28. Actually, I had already been initiated into the graduate program, for I had taken graduate courses in Hebrew, Arabic, and Assyrian with Montgomery and Barton as well as with Margolis and Skoss at Dropsie. I look back on my graduate years (1927–30) in Philadelphia as a period when the standards and scope of Semitic studies left little to be desired. I mention this because a look at the roster of the faculty may give the impression of meagerness. Speiser was on leave in Iraq, leaving only Montgomery (the chairman) and Barton and Chiera on the campus. The *catalogue* for 1927–28 spells out what was expected of the degree candidate: (1) an ability to use French and German publications, and, for biblical courses, also Latin and Greek; (2) in anticipation of Hebrew studies, at least four college units in Hebrew; (3) for M.A. candidates, six graduate units in Semitic linguistic work and a thesis showing proficiency in handling the subject;[5] (4) for Ph.D. candidates, grounding in the elements of the major groups of Semitics (Hebrew, Aramaic, Arabic, Assyrian, Ethiopic, comparative Semitics) and a course in general philology (which meant Professor Roland G. Kent's course on linguistic science), plus a knowledge of the archaeology, history, and literature of the major subject, along with an acquaintance of the whole Semitic field; (5) an understanding that the courses given by the faculty could only partially meet these requirements. These requirements were not merely stated in the Catalogue. They actually reflect the spirit that pervaded the department.

One important change in the faculty occurred in 1928–29. Chiera left

[4] The tablets were published as a University of Pennsylvania doctoral thesis by Speiser's student Jacob Joel Finkelstein, *Cuneiform Texts from Tell Billa* (University of Pennsylvania, 1953).

[5] My M.A. thesis (1928) covered the legal language of the Old Testament. Since court proceedings were conducted in public (often in the city gate), the ancient Hebrew public absorbed legal expressions and used them in everyday speech. Thus the closest approximation to our "in public" is *ba-sha^{c}ar* ("in the gate") in biblical Hebrew.

Penn for Chicago, and Assistant Professor Speiser replaced him. Barton and Speiser handled the Assyriological courses. Speiser's knowledge of linguistics was felt in his Sumerian and Hittite, as well as Akkadian, courses.

Montgomery offered a seminar on text criticism of the book of Kings. It is interesting to note that he refused to give us a course on Daniel, on which his distinguished commentary in the International Critical Commentary series was published in 1927. He explained that he became so sick and tired of Daniel while preparing the commentary that he never wanted to look at the text again. Instead, he taught us Kings, on which his second great commentary would appear a quarter of a century later. Montgomery was thorough and never rushed into print. His first book (on the Samaritans) did not appear until he was forty-one.[6] His subsequent books add up to an impressive contribution of high quality. He was fortunately blessed with good health, a long life, unswerving dedication to his field, and a capacity for work.

In 1929–30, the same faculty as the preceding year continued the program. Montgomery was still concerned with Kings, which is so extensive, and Montgomery's concern with it so deep and many sided, that he gave the course again without duplicating the previous year's offering. This time it was announced as including an introduction to biblical texts and versions. Although archaeological discovery was making its dent on biblical studies, and Montgomery kept abreast of those discoveries, the momentum of the versions and higher criticism was still the main concern of biblical commentators. Montgomery belonged to the era of the International Critical Commentary. Therefore, in his classes (and Margolis's) the student was trained in the ancient translations (Greek, Latin, Aramaic, Syriac) and exposed to a combination of all sorts of daughter versions such as Ethiopic, Coptic, Arabic, Armenian, Georgian, and so forth. Speiser, belonging to the next generation, was eventually to write the commentary on Genesis for tne Anchor Bible series, which laid more emphasis on the discoveries in the Near East, and somewhat less on the ancient versions and commentaries, but, with modifications, still retained a strong emphasis on the documentary analysis in the tradition of nineteenth and early twentieth century higher criticism.

It is worth observing that "South Semitic" (the courses of which were taught by Montgomery and Speiser) now included "Spoken Arabic: The Dialect of Iraq." It will be recalled that Müller had previously taught the modern dialects of Egyptian Arabic, for it was in Egypt that he had his field experience. And now Speiser, who had learned to speak Arabic in the course of his archaeological work in Iraq, was teaching Iraqian

---

[6] *Samaritans: The Earliest Jewish Sect, Their History, Theology and Literature* (Philadelphia: Winston, 1907). This book is essentially his Penn Ph.D. thesis awarded in 1904.

Arabic. This was well before colloquial Semitic languages became familiar in the curricula of universities. What we learned on the campus in
those days was classical Arabic, and we picked up the modern dialects
that we needed in whatever part of the Arabic world we were sent to
explore or excavate. In Iraq we were helped by an excellent book: Van
Ess's *Spoken Arabic of Mesopotamia*,[7] based mainly on the dialect of
Basra, where he served for many years as a missionary. Linguists (like
Kent) stressed the primacy of the spoken word as against the written
word that followed chronologically. Thus, we knew enough to treat
spoken Arabic as a subject in its own right, but we had the valuable
background of classical Arabic, which gave us many advantages. Arabs
respect their classical language and the foreigners who have taken the
trouble to learn Qur'anic and classical literature. Also the classical vo-
cabulary is often understood across modern dialectical lines, whereas
highly colloquial expressions may be intelligible only regionally. Those of
us who were able to converse with the Arabs we worked with in the field
got a precious insight into Near Eastern life before the drastic changes of
the last fifty years, when nationalistic awakening altered for all time the
old way of life. Today, communications (even for the illiterate who have
access to radio and television) have gone far in homogenizing the world.

Speiser also taught the course on comparative semitic grammar, while
Barton and Speiser offered courses on oriental archaeology and history.
Moreover, during this year Barton and Speiser taught Hittite. Barton's
course (like all of his cuneiform courses) had the merit of bringing the
student into direct contact with the cuneiform original.[8] Speiser's had the
additional virtue of disciplining the student in linguistic analysis at a
modern level; in the case of Hittite, this involved comparative Indo-
European grammar.

I took my Ph.D. in June 1930,[9] and stayed on in 1930–31 as an
instructor, teaching graduate courses on Assyrian royal annals and the
Code of Hammurapi as well as undergraduate Hebrew. One of my
students in cuneiform was Zellig Harris, destined to distinguish himself
as a general linguist at the University of Pennsylvania. In my Hebrew
courses at Penn (as later throughout my teaching career on other com-
puses: Johns Hopkins, Smith College, Dropsie College, Brandeis University and New York University), I stressed Margolis's principles of
getting at the underlying laws of the language so as to make the student
independent of the grammar book. In other words, students should have

---

[7] Revised under the title *The Spoken Arabic of Iraq*.

[8] This was true of all my teachers. I never came across university courses on classical or
oriental texts in translation until after my graduate studies were completed.

[9] My Ph.D. thesis is entitled *Rabbinic Exegesis in the Vulgate of Proverbs* (University of
Pennsylvania, 1930; an extract of which was published in *Journal of Biblical Literature* 49
[1930] 384–416).

in their heads the forces that make the language work the way it does, wthout a grammar book in hand. This method requires a familiarity with the Hebrew Bible, which is the ultimate authority on the facts of the language.

In 1930–31, Speiser was on leave in Iraq. Professors Montgomery (chairman), Barton, and Husik were on hand. It was in this year that I was elected a member of the Philadelphia Oriental Club[10] that met monthly for a congenial "collation" and discussing one major and another minor communication by fellow members. The club drew on scholars from several Philadelphia colleges and seminaries as well as from colleges in the Philadelphia area (such as Dropsie College, Bryn Mawr College, Haverford College, Philadelphia Divinity School, Crozer Seminary, Mt. Airy Lutheran Seminary) and even farther afield, from New York to Washington, D.C. There was something built into the Philadelphia Oriental Club that paved the way toward the present scope of the Department of Oriental Studies. The members included Far Eastern scholars, Indo-Iranists, Semitists and Egyptologists. The group members knew each other personally and developed interests in each other's work. As long as terms like "Semitic studies" were used too rigidly, so that "Turkish" had to be sneaked in apologetically, it would be hard to have an oriental department with Chinese, Japanese, southeast Asian languages, Indo-Iranian and Egypto-Semitics. The Club did much to condition the University of Pennsylvania for its present horizons.

It was in 1931–32 that the Department of Oriental Studies was organized as such. During that year, Speiser was directing the excavations at Tell Billa and Tepe Gawra. In the evenings Speiser would read Nuzi tablets with the few of us on the staff who were conversant with cuneiform. I owe my involvement in Nuziana to those evenings in our headquarters in the Yezidi[11] ("devil worshipping") village of Bahshiqa, where we read by the light of kerosene primus lamps. During that year, I also served a short tour of duty with C. Leonard Woolley (1880–1960) at

[10] For the early history of the club, see *Oriental Studies: A Selection of the Papers Read Before the Oriental Club of Philadelphia, 1888–1894* (Boston: Ginn & Company, 1894).

[11] The Yezidis are a sect geared to the propitiation of Satan rather than the worship of God. They believe in God, but since he is exclusively good by nature, there is no purpose in worshiping him. Instead, they propitiate the Prince of Evil, whom they worship under his honorific form the Peacock Angel. They avoid pronouncing the very name *Shaytan* ("Satan") and any word resembling it. While the local Muslims refer to the Tigris as esh-Shatt "The River," the Arabic word for "river" is so close to the forbidden name, that the Yezidis call the Tigris *al-Bahr* "the sea." We had to avoid English expressions like "shut the door" and instead say "close the door."

The Yezidis are Kurds and are a hardy people. Only the village of Bahshiqa, and its nearby sister village of Bahzani, are Arabic speaking. Education is breaking down the old way of life and the Yezidis are becoming an ethnic group with self-awareness and pride rather than a religious community.

Ur as his epigrapher. The excavations there were still yielding jewelry from the many royal Sumerian tombs. The finds were divided among the Iraq Museum in Baghdad, the British Museum in London and the University Museum in Philadelphia. I mention this to bring out the interrelations among the campus staff, the field work, and the University Museum.

I should also note a development outside the University of Pennsylvania that was profoundly to affect the entire Semitics field on every continent. Starting in 1929, the French excavations at Ugarit, on the coast of Syria, unearthed archives of tablets in a new cuneiform alphabet. The atmosphere at Penn had long been such that it could not disregard the Ugaritic tablets that were soon to revolutionize Old Testament philology. Professor Montgomery was to publish some fine pioneering studies on the Ugaritic texts; nor was Professor Barton the kind of person who could resist involvement. Montgomery and his student Zellig Harris collaborated on a preliminary grammar and chrestomathy of Ugaritic. And Ugaritic soon became part of the regular curriculum.

In 1932–33 the graduate school announcement listed the faculty: Montgomery continued as chairman; the professors were Kent, Husik, Hyde, Brown, Legrain, and Speiser. Horace Jayne, Director of the University Museum, is also listed, plus Dr.'s Shryock and Davidson. Catalogues and announcements can be misleading. Thus, while Father Leon Legrain was indeed the Clark Professor of Assyriology, he did not involve himself in teaching. He functioned as curator at the museum. Nor did museum director Jayne teach.

The majors were limited to Indic studies and Semitics. It is true that Dr. Shryock offered courses in Chinese, but the department felt it was not yet ready to embark on a Far Eastern major. The retirement of Professor Barton once more suspended the offerings in Egyptology, though of course the very nature of the department and the museum necessitated its revival. Montgomery offered the courses in Hebrew and Judaistic literature (restricted to the Old Testament, Apocrypha and Pseudepigrapha) and Ethiopic. And jointly with Speiser, he announced courses in first year Arabic and in reading selections from the Arab geographers and historians. Speiser taught Assyrian and Sumerian, but his Hittite course was not offered in 1932–33. Shryock, who was interested in comparative religion as well as Chinese, offered "Outline of Non-Christian Religions." Kent's "General Introduction to Comparative Philology," and "Indo-European Seminary" were now offerings within the department, and not just recommended courses in another department. Rigid linguistic standards were now necessary for the reputable study of all languages at the university level, and although Kent did not go in for the latest linguistic fads, he was the most solid linguist around and no one could provide the student with more discipline and less foolishness. Kent also continued to offer Old Persian, the texts of which are so intricately connected with Mesopotamian, Hebrew, Greek, and Egyptian history. He also gave Avestan. It will be noted that the modern Semitic and Islamic languages are omitted. Modern Hebrew was supplied by extra-curricular instruction, both off campus and on. The need for spoken Arabic was then limited to the staff engaged in archaeology in the field; and Müller's and Speiser's past courses on the dialects of Egypt and Iraq were only straws in the wind. No one was aware that the forces to be unleashed by World War II would eventually evoke a Near Eastern institute in 1965 devoted to modern Arabic, Turkish, and Persian languages and area studies.

Professor Davidson, of the Anthropology Department, gave a course on "The Peoples of Eastern Asia." This reflects a movement to combine archaeology with anthropology. It was still not fully realized that archaeology in the Near East, Iran, India, and China would have to be linked more intimately to philology because the areas were literate from remote antiquity. The University Museum was also engaged in American archaeology where the linkage is properly with the Department of Anthropology. What seems obvious in retrospect is not always clear early on, when new fashions that are legitimate enough in their proper spheres are applied globally.

Husik again offered "History of Jewish Philosophy: Judeo-Alexandrian and Medieval." Whatever the merit of the modern philosophers, their day had not yet come for the department, any more than modern Hebrew Literature, which lay in the future. The final course listed was Sanskirt, elementary and advanced, offered by W. Norman Brown.

The announcement for 1933–34 reflects the back-and-forth movement in trying to make of oriental studies a stable entity. Kent was now the chairman of a division called Indo-European Philology, and Montgomery chaired Oriental Studies, which was staffed by Professors Kent, Husik, Hyde, Brown, Legrain, and Speiser, plus Director Jayne of the museum. Speiser offered a two-year course on "Ancient Oriental History and Cult." The first part (covering from the earliest times to the Amarna period) was omitted in 1933–34; the second part covered from 1500 to 500 B.C. Calling a course on the cuneiform world "Ancient Oriental History and Cult" was a misnomer, now that the department covered oriental studies as far east as China. Changes in coverage and terminology were soon to come. Speiser also was responsible for Mesopotamian and Palestinian archaeology, and Egyptian archaeology was left in limbo.

Professor Hyde, a classicist remembered for his work on athletics in Greece and Rome, taught "Religion and Worship of the Greeks." Although Hyde was not conversant with Semitic and other oriental languages, he was interested in the work of his orientalist colleagues and was a member of the Oriental Club. Moreover, Greek civilization made such an impact on the Near East, that Greek religion was a necessity for areas such as Hellenistic Judaism taught by Montgomery and Husik.

Kent, Husik, and Brown continued their former courses. Montgomery covered biblical Hebrew (teaching Ezekiel) and the "History of the Hebrew Monarchy" (building up to his commentary on Kings). He also offered Syriac, Arabic, and South Arabic. Speiser reintroduced his course on spoken Arabic and announced offerings on Assyriology, including Sumerian and, for the first time, Elamite. Elamite (it will be recalled) was one of the official languages on the trilingual inscriptions of the Achaemenian Empire. But although the Old Persian opened up the Babylonian on the trilinguals, the decipherment of Elamite had lagged because it is not related to any well-known family of languages. But the very offering of Elamite exemplifies the Pennsylvania tradition of probing into the problematic byways of scholarship while fostering a deep commitment to the mainstream.

The academic year 1934–35 witnessed much the same program. It should be noted that Speiser resumed his Hittite course using Edgar Sturtevant's *Hittite Grammar*. Sturtevant was an Indo-Europeanist. Cuneiform Hittite has been fostered by two entirely different types of scholars: cuneiformists who handle the texts, and Indo-Europeanists who place Hittite within the framework of the other Indo-European languages. Speiser kept abreast of both camps.

The offerings for 1935–36 were much the same. The important innovation was Montgomery's "The Hebraic Ras Shamra Texts." Montgomery, entering his seventieth year and nearing retirement, had the ability and will to embark on this new field, so full of pitfalls as well as challenges. It is noteworthy that Montgomery's published contributions to Ugaritic (Ras Shamra) studies were not only courageous but good.

The stressing of Hurrian by Speiser in the curriculum begins in 1936–37. Hurrian is an important strand in the fabric of the ancient Near East and Speiser's *Introduction to Hurrian* is one of the major publications in the field. It might be noted that Hurrian is related linguistically only to Urartean, the language of Urartu (Ararat) before that country became Armenia, and was populated by the Indo-European Armenians. Hurrian texts have been found in Amarna, Boghazkeui, Ugarit, and a host of other sites. The majority of the inhabitants of Nuzi was Hurrian, as were large minorities at Alalakh and Ugarit. But when new categories of Hurrian tablets are found we still have great difficulty making sense of them. This is another way of saying that there is still a need for a handbook of Hurrian that will enable a qualified student to understand Hurrian texts rather than just teach linguistic details.

The advent of Dr. Zellig Harris marks the scene in 1937–38. His 1934 Ph.D. dissertation at Penn, written under Montgomery's guidance, is the still useful *Grammar of the Phoenician Language* (1936).[12] And in 1939 his monograph, *The Development of the Canaanite Dialects*, demonstrated his command of Semitics. The announcement for 1937–38 has Dr. Harris teaming up with Montgomery to teach Hebrew, Ugaritic, Syriac, Aramaic, Arabic, South Arabic, and Ethiopic, while it has Harris joining Speiser to offer comparative Semitic grammar, Phoenician and West Semitic, Spoken Arabic, and Assyriology, including a seminar on the Nuzi tablets. Speiser also offered courses on Hurrian and Elamite.

Except for the advent of Professor Hermann Ranke, 1938–39 was much the same as the preceding year. In his younger days at Penn Ranke produced an opus on Babylonian personal names. By now he had switched his energies to Egyptology, and it is worth noting that one of his contributions to the field is his standard work on Egyptian personal names now in its second edition. Visitors from Nazi Germany, beginning with Ranke, were to bring some of the cream of oriental scholarship to the Department of Oriental Studies at Penn. Since Barton's retirement, Egyptian instruction has been set on the backburner, even though an able British Egyptologist, Battiscombe Gunn, had filled in as curator of the Egyptian section of the museum during the midthirties. Ranke announced two courses for 1938–39: "Introduction to Egyptian" (based on Erman's Egyptian grammar, fourth German edition, even though Gardiner's *Egyptian Grammar*, which has the virtues of being more extensive as well as in English, had been available since 1927) and a seminar in Egyptian texts. In order to pull the Oriental Studies Department together, the entire staff offered a lecture course, "Interconnections of Early Oriental Civilizations."

The outbreak of World War II occurred in 1939. For the department, it marked the close of Montgomery's active career. He devoted his remaining years to preparing his commentary on Kings. He lived to know that it would see the light of day. A disciple, Professor Henry S. Gehman,[13]

---

[12] Published also as volume 8 of the American Oriental Series.

[13] Gehman was Pennsylvania Dutch from Lancaster County, Pennsylvania. He never got over his "Dutch" accent, which made him sound like a foreigner. At a Princeton reception, a society lady asked him: "And when did you come to this country?" He retorted: "In the seventeenth century."

He had taken his Ph.D. in Indology under Kent, who would not raise a finger to place him. For years, Gehman had to teach languages (mainly Spanish) in high school, but he never abandoned the hope of a scholarly career. Eventually he decided to switch to the Old Testament field under Montgomery. Though Gehman was twenty years older than I, we were trained in the same classes. Since he already had a Ph.D. he took an S.T.D. (Doctor of Sacred Theology) at the Philadelphia Divinity School, for Montgomery was professor there as well as at Penn. Under Montgomery, Gehman became an expert in textual criticism and got the professorship in Old Testament at Princeton Theological Seminary. Simultaneously he taught Semitics in the Department of Oriental Languages and Literatures at Princeton University. For years he was the classical Semitist of Princeton University in a period when the departmental emphasis was on the contemporary

promised to see it through publication. It was published in 1951 after Montgomery's death on 6 February 1949.

Several scholars, who were active during the Montgomery years, merit remembrance. Professor George Aaron Barton (1859–1942) was a Canadian of Quaker persuasion. During World War I, he openly supported the war effort of Great Britain and the Allies. Therefore, he had to break with the peace-loving Society of Friends. Thereafter he became, and remained for life, an Episcopalian priest. He took his Ph. D. (at Harvard) under David Gordon Lyon,[14] who had been trained in Assyriology in Germany. Lyon then returned to the United States where he, as America's first native Assyriologist, came to be known as the "Father of American Assyriology." As a student of Barton's, I am in the second generation of cuneiformists born and trained in America.

Barton had remarkable breadth and perspective, though he was less impressive in methodology. At a testimonial dinner given in 1939 to honor him and celebrate his eightieth birthday, he insisted that, while he did not begrudge any orientalist his particular brand of linguistics, he (Barton) was entitled, in a free world, to his own kind of linguistics. This cavalier approach to methodological discipline limited Barton's performance as a scholar and teacher. Fortunately, when I was his student, other teachers provided the requisite linguistic and philological principles. I refer particularly to his colleagues Roland Kent, James Montgomery, and Ephraim Speiser.

Barton had a robust sense of humor. He told us of a hillbilly named Joshua, who, when asked in court by the judge whether he was the Joshua who had made the sun stand still, replied: "No, Your Honor, I'm the Joshua who made the moonshine still." In archaeology class, a student asked what a "rhyton" was. Barton asked to see the reference. It was the title of a photographic illustration in the text. Upon being shown the picture, Barton said: "Well, that's one of them, isn't it?" Although he

---

Near East. Gehman approached scholarship with the seriousness of a "Dutch" farmer. Though unimaginative, he was solid and thorough, with no time for nonsense. His students respected and feared him. He initiated first-year seminarians with a direct order to memorize the names and dates of all the kings of Israel and Judah. This served notice on the budding theologians that they would have to burn midnight oil to qualify in Old Testament.

[14] David Gordon Lyon (1852–1935) received his Ph. D. from the University of Leipzig in 1882 and in the same year became Hollis Professor of Divinity at Harvard. He concentrated on Assyriology, and his *Assyrian Manual* (1886) was quite useful in its time. Forty years later, his student George Barton was still using Lyon's *Manual* when it was already quite antiquated. And in 1958, when another disciple of Lyon's (Robert H. Pfeiffer, 1892–1958) died, and I took over his Assyrian course at Harvard, the textbook was still Lyon's *Manual!* In using the *Manual*, Barton and Pfeiffer were loyal to their Assyriological "father". *Malgré moi*, I taught Assyrian from Lyon's *Manual* in 1958, walking in the footsteps of my Assyriological "grandfather".

led an exemplary life, his jokes sometimes bordered on the burlesque. He told us of a professor who asked a waitress: "How's the chicken today?" to which she replied: "Fine, kid! How's yourself?"

Barton acquainted us with fields like Egypto-Semitics at a time when his more sedate colleagues shied away from all but the well-beaten paths. For the judicious student, he opened new horizons.

When we read the Gudea cylinders, we compared all the published translations with a view to coming up with a still different interpretation. Barton sought originality and encouraged it in us. What he did not fully realize was that the primary goal of sound interpretation is not originality but the rediscovery of the original author's intent.

In Assyriology, his method was particularly chaotic. The script is so full of polyphony and homophony that the scholar must never forget that the task is to get at the author's meaning and not to *épater la bourgeoisie*. Barton was fond of using his own monograph entitled *Babylonian Writing*, which aims at listing all the values of each sign. Let us say that a three-sign word starts with a symbol of 10 different values, followed by one of 20 values, and concludes with one of 15 values. This means that there are 3000 ($= 10 \times 20 \times 15$) conceivable ways of reading the word. Instead of insisting that we seek the correct original sense in accordance with strict methods, Barton urged the student to come up with a *new* one. As a result, a gifted student, destined to become a leading Sumerologist, Samuel Noah Kramer, was confusd and turned off by Barton's instruction and had to wait until, in the following decade, he was set on the right course, by Arno Poebel at Chicago, toward a distinguished career in Sumerian literature. Poebel had formulated the grammar of Sumerian in 1923.

Barton's industry was phenomenal. In addition to a heavy teaching load, his publication output was huge. His *Archaeology and the Bible* (7th ed., revised, 1937) was not only a popular success but was based on the original sources. His International Critical Commentary volume on Ecclesiastes (1908) gave him a place in Old Testament studies. His *History of the Hebrew People* (1930) aimed at telling the course of Israel's experience down to 70 A.D. largely in the words of the biblical authors. His copies of cuneiform texts give him a lasting place in Assyriology. From his *Religions of the World* (3d ed., 3d printing, 1935) to his *A Sketch of Semitic Origins* (1902), there were all sorts of fields that he covered in the manner of a renaissance man.

He never missed a class, even though his health was far from perfect. Between classes he used to whisk out and consume little bottles of Grape Nuts and milk because dyspepsia obliged him to eat "little but often." Though his hands shook from a tremor, he continued to copy texts. He refused to be stopped by obstacles.

His first marriage to a recluse named Carrie protected him from the world so that he could study and write prolifically. Their house was virtually closed to the world; rarely did anyone get past the front door. The shades were pulled down and the interior was dark and dusty. In the late twenties, his wife died and Dr. Barton's secretary, Katherine Blye Hagy, took over. She saw to it that the home was cleared of dust and became accessible with sunlight shining through the windows. Wedding bells would soon be ringing. Professor Montgomery hailed the marriage as Barton's reward for so many years of patience with his first wife. Since Dr. Barton was already old, and his bride was on the threshold of middle age, parental permission was hardly necessary for sanctioning the nuptials. For reasons unknown to me, the couple eloped to Elkton, Maryland, to be joined in holy matrimony by the notorious "marrying parson" who performed quick weddings often for inebriated couples during the prohibition era. The results were predictable and immediate; the press got hold of the story and the Philadelphia papers carried headlines like "Prof. Elopes to Elkton with Secretary." It is not always what we do but sometimes how we do it that matters.

The newlyweds tried living during the winters in a trailer in Florida and during the summers in their home in Weston, Massachusetts. I visited them occasionally in Weston, and after 1956, when I began to teach at nearby Brandeis University, I was in close contact with Mrs. Barton, who after Dr. Barton's death, was married to Mr. Beach Platt, the widower next door. She gave me some of Barton's memorabilia such as religious objects he had purchased in the Holy Land, including a piece of "Noah's Ark" and a fragment of the "true cross." Barton shared Mark Twain's estimate of such relics, and they keep reminding me of Barton's rollicking sense of humor. The academic problems in Barton's day included the battle between Egyptologists and Assyriologists: Which civilization was the older? At a learned society meeting a protagonist of Egypt got up and proclaimed: "Egyptian priority is obvious from the pyramids." Barton retorted: "The Mesopotamians invented the wheel, and in Western civilization, we used wheels a lot more than pyramids."

Barton had perspective. He was no Thureau-Dangin in Assyriology, nor a Gardiner in Egyptology, but unlike the other generalists, he knew enough of both fields to make legitimate comparisons. It should not be lost on the reader that Barton's estimate of the situation has prevailed. I owe something to Barton. In an atmosphere of cautious and often timid scholarship, he set an example of courageous, broad probing. Humankind does not live by pedantry alone.

James A. Montgomery (1866–1949) was a quite different man. He was the only aristocratic scholar and gentleman among my teachers. Descended from distinguished Philadelphians on both sides, he looked regal. Tall and gaunt, he cut an imposing figure. Quite dolichocephalic, his head was reminiscent of St. Jerome's by El Greco. He also bore a striking resemblance to the mummy of Ramses II. His extended family included men like Viscount Field Marshal Montgomery and Bishop Montgomery of Tasmania.

He was a devout Christian and Episcopalian priest; but his deepest commitment was to Old Testament scholarship. He respected traditional Jewish learning and assumed that I knew a lot more about Hebraica and Judaica than I actually did. His expectations spurred me on to greater efforts, for I would not disappoint my master. When I accepted his suggestion that I write on the rabbinic influences on Jerome's writings, he and I were echoing a precious historic process: the collaboration of Christians and Jews in probing the meaning of the Scriptures they shared and cherished.

Montgomery did not want his three sons to follow in his footsteps professionally because of the economic hardship that so often besets scholars. He warned me of the financial difficulties that might (and eventually did) befall me, but when I assured him that Semitic scholarship was, for better or for worse, the only acceptable way of life for me, he did not raise the subject again and always treated me as a son as well as disciple. Our mutual devotion was, to the very end, total, untainted with the love-hate ambivalence that so often characterizes parent-child and teacher-student relations.

Montgomery was on the threshold of old age when I first became his student in the mid 1920s. Though at the height of his career in terms of productivity, he had become quite absentminded. In our Bible seminar, there were about half a dozen students, all white except a Dr. Young, who was black. Montgomery had the habit of looking up at a corner of the ceiling while addressing the class. Dr. Young specialized in the Vetus Latina and one day, when Dr. Young happened to be absent, Montgomery addressed a long soliloquy on the Vetus Latina to Dr. Young. When Montgomery at last posed a question to Young, we informed our master of Young's absence. Montgomery groaned, "Oh, oh!"

In Syriac class, Kramer and I were the only students reading *Kalilag wa-Dimnag* with Montgomery. In those days a favorite radio program was "Amos 'n Andy," a white team that impersonated two amusing blacks. In our text Kalilag and Dimnag were two talking jackals. Montgomery raised his eyes from the text and asked us, "Gentlemen! Don't they remind you of Andrew and Amos?"

He was moderate but not abstinent. He enjoyed smoking and told me that since he had not begun to smoke until he was well beyond the usual starting age, there was still hope for me to learn and cultivate the pleasure. This was one of the few areas in which I did not emulate the master.

He was stately and vigorous. His gait was so rapid that it was hard to keep up with him. He never owned a car so that he got lots of exercise

walking between the Thirtieth Street Railroad Station and the Philadelphia Divinity School or University of Pennsylvania where he held his
classes. He did not like to speak foreign languages, preferring to allow a
foreign visitor to speak his own language, and Montgomery would answer
in English.

In spite of two full teaching jobs (he was professor at both the University of Pennsylvania and the Philadelphia Divinity School simultaneously), he spent much time at home working on his publications
during weekends, evenings, and summers. He counted on the summers
also for preparing new courses for the coming academic year. His files
were at home, not in his offices. His adoring wife ran their large, gracious
home and protected him from distractions. In those days, scholars like
Montgomery lived in genteel simplicity and there were few temptations
to make money lecturing all over the country. Airplanes were not in
general use and it took too long to travel long distances by train to accept
frequent lecture engagements in America's many cities between the
Atlantic and Pacific.

Montgomery had no time for mental or physical frailties. In my first
year as a graduate student, I noted that a peculiar phonetic correspondence in the Semitic languages was identical with one observed in a
journal of psychology in an article on an insane patient. I showed my
finding to Montgomery and asked if I should write it up for publication.
He replied with an emphatic "no!" and advised me to confine my
interests to sane subjects.

On my greeting him with a routine "How are you?" he said: "My dear
boy, if you hadn't asked me, I would have given it no thought." He was
uninterested in complaints about health or any expression of what you
could or could not eat or drink. Such topics he found boring and of no
interest to anyone. When he was in his early sixties, I referred to a
certain professor as "old doctor So-and-so." "Be careful, young man," he
admonished me, "he is my classmate and contemporary." Montgomery
taught me to think healthy and think young.

Montgomery received the respect he deserved: honorary degrees,
presidencies of learned societies, and so forth. He accepted all such
honors modestly. He was a true scholar and gentleman: an *avis rara* in
his time, and a still rarer bird today.

Something must be said of two Semitists who, though not directly
associated with Penn, were inextricably part of the same picture: Max
Margolis of Dropsie and William Albright of Johns Hopkins. Max
Leopold Margolis (1866–1932), Professor of Biblical Philology at Dropsie
College, was my most effective teacher. Rather homely, and with a far
from pleasant voice, he lacked charm—at least on the surface. Coming
from a background of enlightened Lithuanian Jews, he was born and bred
to be a scholar, dedicated to learning for its own sake. He was taught both

Hebrew and the classical languages from an early age and was sent to Germany for his high school *(Gymnasium)* education. Migrating to America in 1889, he took his Ph. D. at Columbia in 1891 under Richard Gottheil and wrote his thesis in Latin on a rabbinic subject. In 1897 he became Assistant Professor in Semitics at the University of California at Berkeley and was later promoted to Associate Professor. There he married Evelyn Kate Aronson, who bore him three children: a girl and twin boys.

A higher salary was among the factors that induced him to accept in 1905 a professorship in biblical exegesis at Hebrew Union College in Cincinnati. There his Zionism brought him into conflict with the then anti-Zionist attitude of Reform Judaism and he was soon without a job. Twenty years later Margolis told me that the greatest mistake he ever made was leaving the University of California for Hebrew Union College. Fortunately, Dropsie College was soon to be opened and the president, Cyrus Adler, chose him to be Professor of Biblical Philology. In the interim he accepted an invitation to Germany where he wrote his superb *Manual of the Aramaic Language of the Babylonian Talmud* (Munich, 1910).

Margolis exemplified the principle that a serious humanist spends his time reading and understanding the original texts of his specialty. He knew the secondary literature well, and his library, located in his office where he conducted his seminars, was a model of quality and orderliness. But, for him, the ultimate authority was the primary source.

His greatest strength lay in his mastery of the text and linguistic analysis of the Hebrew Old Testament. An intimate knowledge of the text was basic, and a student who did not recognize the book and chapter of any biblical verse was often told, "Go to hell!" He was not suave, but he meant no harm in cursing students. The fact was, he liked students who would take his verbal abuse in stride. Once, when President Adler had told him not to send students to hell, Margolis asked me: "Don't you think such language adds to the informality of my classes?"

Margolis stressed the fundamentals of Hebrew, which he understood and formulated, as no one else did. Much of the inflexion results mechanically from the effects of syllabification and accent. What the standard grammars take hundreds of pages to explain, Margolis reduced to formulae and charts that can be put on a couple of ordinary sheets of paper. A disciple, when fully exposed to Margolis's methods, did not need a grammar book; the principles were lodged in memory. Margolis knew the value of reference books, but he also knew that they could never take the place of ready knowledge. He used to say: "In the candy store, you must lay a coin on the counter. You cannot say 'I have money in the bank'". The definitions of words had to depend on their context in specific passages in the literature; the authority of dictionaries was relegated to the category of secondary sources.

Margolis's ongoing research project was the attempt to get at the "Ur-Septuaginta" for the sake of determining what Hebrew text lay before the Ptolemaic translators. The evidence of the Dead Sea Scrolls shows how futile this task can be. And I suspect that deep down inside, Margolis sensed this. One of his aphorisms was: "A bad original is better than a good translation." He knew that a corrupt Hebrew manuscript was closer to the original than the best translations. On occasion he grew weary from collating versions and daughter versions. On deciding not to pursue some tertiary manuscript, he would lay down his pencil and say, "There is an end to slavishness." What I am implying is that he was committed to his vast project beyond the point of retreat; but he was plagued with doubts of a basic nature.

Many of his sayings are memorable. He pointed out that most of what we know is common knowledge for which we cannot take personal credit. He would accordingly warn us: "As your knowledge is corporate, make sure that your ignorance is corporate, and not private." One of Margolis's frustrations was that he lacked the external charm of his brother Rabbi Elias Margolis. Max Margolis took this frustration out on those of his students who were rabbis. Since he believed in Zionism and felt that the Diaspora was doomed, he would tell the rabbis: "Your *bamot* (Pagan "highplaces") will never keep Judaism alive." I used to eat lunch with him in his office. On one such occasion, he remarked: "If all the rabbis were put on a transatlantic liner, and it were sunk in midocean by an aerial bomb, the world would be the better for it."

His bark was worse than his bite. Actually he was infinitely kind and patient with students dedicated to learning. An intelligent comment on the part of even a young student would evoke his immediate commendation. And he respected real scholars and real gentlemen—but they had to be the real thing. He did not suffer fools or knaves gladly.

He was highly respected during his lifetime, but now that more than half a century has passed since his death, he is only beginning to get the credit he deserves. His writings reflect only a small part of his contributions. His profound mastery of biblical philology came through more fully in his teaching. Great teaching is not accomplished through books so much as through intimate classroom contact over a period of years. Very few of Margolis's students were capable of absorbing enough of his mastery to carry on the tradition. I like to think that it has not only been the most valuable discipline I have received but also that I have transmitted it to three generations of students who carry it on and add to it.

Margolis and his family spent 1924–25 in Palestine, where he was the annual professor at the American School of Oriental Research in Jerusalem. He also taught at Hebrew University, which officially opened in 1925. In Palestine, he went on a memorable field trip with the young William Albright. The two men respected each other enormously. Albright saw in Margolis a matchless scholar whose command of the Greek renditions of Hebrew place names in the book of Joshua shed unique light on the topography of the Holy Land. Margolis saw in Albright a brilliant luminary in Palestinology.

That year brought sorrow to Margolis. One of his twin boys was smitten with fever and died. Margolis never got over his tragic loss. The body of the child was transported to Philadelphia for burial. Every sabbath eve, Margolis mourned at his son's grave.

Like Socrates, Margolis never thought he had founded a "school of thought." We know that Socrates was a great teacher who founded an immortal "school of thought" only by what has emerged since he died. Margolis was the greatest master and teacher of biblical philology of our century. That he indeed established a great school of thought in his field has become evident only since his death. A school of thought is not the same as a school of fish. Many a pompous savant is deceived into imagining that a mob of brainwashed followers constitutes a school of thought whereas it is more akin to a school of fish.

The rising star on the horizon of Near Eastern scholarship during my formative years was William Foxwell Albright (1891–1971) of Johns Hopkins University. In addition to research, writing, and teaching, he was active on the field staff and governing board of the American Schools of Oriental Research in Jerusalem and Baghdad. He was at the height of his intellectual powers when I began to work with him in 1931. I spent 1931–35 with him intermittently in the field, and in 1935–38 I served as his teaching fellow at Johns Hopkins.

Succeeding his mentor, Paul Haupt, in Baltimore, he strengthened his base at Johns Hopkins, which he never left. Tempting offers came his way, such as a name professorship at Yale, but he was never seriously tempted to leave Johns Hopkins. He strengthened his position by taking over the editorship of BASOR (Bulletin of the American Schools of Oriental Research), in which he promptly made his own contributions to current discoveries and developments in Near Eastern archaeology. He also used BASOR to get back at his critics promptly.

Montgomery had wide knowledge and broad historic perspective, but he lacked Albright's boldness and flamboyance. Montgomery recognized that Albright could handle the sources of his many interests and therefore could not be dismissed as a mere synthesizer or generalist. But he expressed his misgivings to me laconically: "The trouble with Albright is that he knows too much."

Albright respected meticulous, specific scholarship. While I was studying with Margolis in the late twenties, Albright called on him to discuss the topography of the book of Joshua, for Margolis was preparing his monumental edition of the Septuagint version of Joshua. The two men, while so different in their work and temperaments, respected each other profoundly.

I was with Albright (1931–35) during the final period of his heavy involvement in field archaeology. My first assignment was at Beth-Zur in the summer of 1931. We lived simply in tents. In those days, the University of Chicago, flush with Rockefeller funding, exemplified "splendor-in-the-field." The expedition at Megiddo not only functioned expertly on a grand scale, but provided its staff with tennis courts and hot tub baths.

Albright was the son of an impecunious Methodist missionary. William was born in Chile, where his parents were endeavoring to convert Catholics into Methodists. Those early years left indelible impressions on the scholar-to-be. First, his English pronunciation always bore the stamp of the Spanish he had spoken as a child. Second, he remained uncompromisingly loyal to the Methodist Church, and it irritated him to hear that people incorrectly assumed he had converted to Catholicism because his wife and four sons had. Last, Albright never got over the poverty of his youth. He practiced parsimony as a way of life and, while doing important work on a shoestring, he privately criticized the extravagance of the University of Chicago's Oriental Institute. His attitude unfortunately took the form of imposing substandard salaries on his protegés. It must be added that in other matters, Albright was often generous— especially with his time.

On expeditions, he would spend hours every day with the younger men on the staff to explain the strata and phases of the excavation. He would be infinitely patient in examining potshards with us, inducting us into the most meticulous ceramic research of the day—particularly at Tell Beit Mirsim where he established a classic chronology of the pottery.

He was afraid of women and did not want them on his field staff. He readily acknowledged the ability of women archaeologists like Dorothy Garrod, Kathleen Kenyon, Hetty Goldman, and many other distinguished women excavators, but he did not want women—young or old—on his digs.

His likes and dislikes had amusing effects on his scholarship. He abominated camels and adored donkeys. This had a subconscious effect on his pronouncements and publications concerning the patriarchal age. He "got rid" of the camels by turning their very mention in the patriarchal narratives into anachronisms. His love of the donkey impelled him to stress the role of the Fathers as donkey caravaneers.

Albright had an inordinate fondness for snakes—dead or alive. On one occasion he picked up the sloughed-off skin of a snake and held it up with affection. This predilection went hand-in-hand with his discovery that in the eleventh tablet of the Epic of Gilgamesh the serpent's sloughed-off skin betokened the rejuvenation that the snake acquired through stealing the elixir of youth from Gilgamesh.

His knowledge of Palestinian topography and the ceramics of the individual sites was uncanny. One Sunday, a few of us younger members of the staff took a field trip into the Judean wilderness. He suggested we go to Tell Arad, Tell el-Milḥ, and another mound in that vicinity and bring back a bag of surface shards from each of the three sites. We did so, and without a moment's hesitation, he identified the source of each bag correctly.

The expedition meals were unforgettable because of his conversation. It was at Beth-Zur in 1931 that he dropped the following remark that significantly shaped my subsequent career: "Every student of the Old Testament would do well to work on Ugaritic." At that time, Ugaritic was in the initial stages of being interpreted. I attribute my subsequent dedication to Ugaritic to the impact of Albright's remark. He foresaw the inevitability of Ugarit's importance.

In 1933, the uprising of the Assyrian Christians and their consequent massacre at the hands of the Iraqian army, were part of a chaotic interlude in the history of Iraq. The excavations of the American School of Oriental Reserarch in Baghdad were suspended for the year (1933–34), which gave me the opportunity to accompany Albright for winter assignments, including his brief but memorable excavations at Ader, in trans-Jordan.

In the spring of 1935, I was notified that for the following year my salary would be reduced to zero but that I would be "the first Albert T. Clay Fellow of the American School of Oriental Research in Baghdad": an "honor" that I would not dignify with an acknowledgment, for it was only a euphemism for the academic demise that Ephraim Speiser had planned for me. It was Albright who thwarted Speiser by taking me under his wing and retaining me at Johns Hopkins as a teaching fellow from 1935 to 1938. At Hopkins, Albright was now devoting himself to teaching and research. He soon became the world's foremost mentor for doctoral students in Near Eastern studies.

He then had no secretary and typed all of his manuscripts and correspondence. His office door was always open and any student could barge in to present a new idea. Albright would then drop what he was doing, listen attentively, and make suggestions. Thereafter, he would return to whatever he had been doing without requiring any time for readjusting.

During 1937–38, I suggested to Alfred Pohl, S.J., the editor of *Orientalia* and *Analecta Orientalia*, that I prepare a grammar of Ugaritic for the latter series. He conferred with his colleagues who joined with him enthusiastically in advocating the project. While it was Albright who inspired me to undertake the task, it was the training I had received under Margolis that enabled me to perform it. Albright had breadth of vision, whereas Margolis had drummed into me the detailed principles of Northwest Semitic linguistics. I did not consult anyone on whether or how I should perform the task and my Pontifical Biblical Institute friends did not meddle. They left the authorship to me, and I left the publishing to them. When the production of the *Ugaritic Grammar* was already underway, I informed Albright. He was furious and informed me in no uncertain way that my plan was not only presumptuous but impossible: no one could do it in the foreseeable future. I realized then and there that Baltimore was no longer big enough for the two of us and I moved to Smith College in the fall of 1938.

I must say to Albright's credit that when my *Ugaritic Grammar* appeared, he admitted in print that he had been wrong in trying to dissuade me from undertaking the project. Moreover, he hailed the opus as an achievement of singular importance. Albright was nearly always big enough to confess his mistakes.

Albright ended his career as the outstanding authority on the biblical world. He had overwhelmed the opposition by his versatility. He could crush philologians by changing the subject to archaeology and silence the archaeologists by shifting the discussion to the written sources. He had many disciples whom he could, and often did, stir up to pounce on his critics.

My identification of Minoan Linear A as Northwest Semitic is probably the most important breakthrough of my career. I published it without consulting Albright or anyone else. When it was a fait accompli, he opposed it, not with valid arguments, but by casting doubts—such as, that others did not approve of it either. I reacted strongly and expressed the hope that he would exercise his well-known virtue of retracting his mistakes. His devotees blindly assumed that he knew everything about everything. As a product of Margolis's discipline, I not only knew Hebrew and Northwest Semitic grammar better than Albright, but I knew that I knew it. There is no doubt that the acceptance of my identification of Minoan would have come much sooner, had I swallowed my pride and did what other more politic scholars had done: come to Albright humbly, flattered him, explained the facts, and begged for his support. He, after all, was the opinion maker par excellence. I paid the price for not appealing to him, but I was constitutionally unable to act otherwise. Truth, in the world of self-respecting scholarship, should not require the endorsement of celebrities. Academia should be different from Madison Avenue. But that is not the way the world functions.

Now that Albright has entered the academy on high, I can evaluate and express my indebtedness to him *sine studio et ira*. From James

Montgomery, I learned what it means to be a scholar and gentleman. Max Margolis taught me meticulous philology applied to Hebrew and cognate languages. William Albright exposed me to breadth of vision and combinatory Near Eastern studies. There were other influential teachers in my life—but Montgomery, Margolis and Albright were the "big three."

5.   THE WAR YEARS

World War II brought on added awareness that all humankind belongs to "one world." This now sounds trite, but in 1939–40 it was a radical concept in isolationistic America, particularly in the Middle West, which was geographically remote from both the Atlantic and Pacific Oceans. The people along the east coast were often well aware of Europe, and those along the west coast, of the Far East.

While Speiser was destined in the long run to carry on the Semitic tradition at Penn, he did get caught up in the whirlwind of war fever and worked on Near Eastern affairs for the Office of Strategic Services. Brown became the chairman of the department of Oriental Studies (1939–48) for the war years, but he too was involved in Washington, not only in the affairs of India but also of Southeast Asia. Federal funds became increasingly available for area and linguistic training on the campuses, and for the services of orientalists in Washington as well as in various theaters of operation abroad.

The war years saw a demand for orientalists in the armed forces and civilian agencies concerned directly or indirectly with the war effort. This went hand in hand with the flight of classically oriented students from the campuses, along with the influx of government-sponsored trainees for military and civilian agencies.

In 1939–40, the presence of Assistant Professor Bodde to teach Chinese was "in the national interest" as our increased involvement in Pacific affairs grew. Assistant Professor Harris played a role in government-sponsored instruction in Arabic dialects, based on reconstructing a language from the utterances of an informant who was a native speaker of the local dialect.[1] Harris was becoming more and more interested in lin-

[1] This technique was originally designed for analyzing the speech of "primitive" people who have no tradition of writing. But to apply it in universities to varieties of Arabic (the medium of a great literature) is another matter. I was approached to participate in such an Arabic training program in Washington but I declined. My reason was simply that a standard Arabic would open the door to all the dialects, whereas learning the speech of, let us say, a blacksmith in Casablanca would not be the right way to train Americans to cope with the varieties of Arabic speech they would be exposed to if they moved on from a Moroccan port to Tunisia and beyond. A well-known linguist published his analysis of Turkish based on an informant. The numerous Arabic loanwords were not treated as Arabic but as anomalous forms.

I see no merit in not knowing the origin of the Arabic borrowings into Turkish, which again is no "primitive" language but instead the medium of an extensive literature. The methods we adopt or create must fit the problem under consideration. Analyzing the

guistic theory, and he eventually formed his own linguistic department, divorced from Semitics, and achieved acclaim in linguistics. He is now (1986) Emeritus Benjamin Franklin Professor of Linguistics at Penn.

Visiting Professor Ranke was now offering three courses in Egyptian. The introductory courses were based on Erman's grammar, fourth edition, while the second year course followed Alan Gardiner's more detailed and technical *Egyptian Grammar*. A seminar in Egyptian texts was also announced.[2]

In 1940–41, two distinguished visiting professors adorned the department: Ranke and Giorgio Levi della Vida. Levi della Vida was one of eleven professors in Italy who refused to take the fascist oath and therefore lost their posts. A loyal Italian scholar and gentleman from a prominent Venetian family (the Palazzo Levi della Vida is on the Grand Canal), he preferred exile to paying lip service to the duce. He is among the great Arabists of our century but was also accomplished in Northwest Semitic. He taught "Religion of the Western Semites," and the "Introduction to Islamic Religion and History." Along with Harris, he offered Hebrew, Islamic religion and history, Ugaritic, Syriac and Aramaic, South Arabic, and Ethiopic. No less than three Arabic courses were listed to meet the needs of elementary, intermediate, and advanced students. It is obvious that not all these courses could have been given simultaneously. Moreover, the war had begun to drain off students from such classical and ancient studies.

Speiser and Harris jointly offered courses in Semitic linguistics, comparative Semitic grammar, Northwest Semitic, spoken Arabic and Assyriology. One of Harris's courses deserves special mention because it anticipated future developments. Harris had been raised in a Philadelphia home where the parents and children conversed fluently in Hebrew. It should be remembered that Israel had not yet become a state, but Palestine, then under the British mandate, had many speakers of Hebrew in the cities, towns, and agricultural settlements. Back in 1925, Hebrew University had been established, reflecting the intellectual side of the revival of Hebrew as a fait accompli before statehood was won in 1948. Jewish groups on and off the University of Pennsylvania campus fostered spoken Hebrew, but until Harris offered Modern Hebrew in 1940–41, it was not part of the academic curriculum.

The emphasis of the Montgomery era on ancient texts continued. But

---

speech of an illiterate American Indian tribe is one thing; analyzing Arabic, Turkish, or English, quite another.

[2] One of Ranke's students in Egyptology at Penn was the linguist Carleton Taylor Hodge (1917–   ), whose thesis, however, *An Outline of Hausa Grammar*, was under the supervision of Harris. (University of Pennsylvania, 1947; published in *Language*, dissertation 41, a publication of the Linguistic Society of America.)

now we see the teaching of modern Semitic dialects (Hebrew as well as Arabic), which anticipated the present mood. Montgomery spoke neither Arabic nor Hebrew (nor had his predecessors in the great tradition, including even Nöldeke, who, like many other great orientalists, had never even visited the Near East!). The only prominent non-Jewish Hebraists who were fluent in Hebrew before World War II were William F. Albright of Johns Hopkins and Canon Herbert Danby[3] of St. George's (Episcopal) Cathedral in Jerusalem, later to become Regius Professor of Hebrew at Oxford University. Today there are thousands of non-Jews (scholars and laity) who are fluent in Hebrew, including some who write books and articles in Hebrew.

Speiser continued to offer Sumerian, Elamite, and Hurrian. Ranke announced a full program in Egyptian: introductory Egyptian, second year Egyptian, a seminar in Egyptian texts, hieratic texts, and Coptic texts.

In 1941–42 (under the chairmanship of Brown), Ranke, Levi della Vida, Speiser, and Harris offered pretty much the same array of courses. During that year the bombing of Pearl Harbor on 7 December 1941 changed world history, including Semitic studies at the University of Pennsylvania.

In 1942–43, Levi della Vida is "Professor" (and no longer "Visiting Professor"). We mention this to show that his subsequent return to Italy after the war was entirely his own choice. As far as the University of Pennsylvania was concerned, he was a permanent, tenured professor. On the other hand, Ranke remained a "Visiting Professor."

The *Announcement for 1943–44* omits any reference to Ranke, but notes the addition of two lecturers: Liebesny and Wieschoff. Brown was still chairman, and Professors Levi della Vida, Kent, and Speiser, as well as Associate Professor Harris and Assistant Professor Bodde were there for their accustomed courses. Professor Legrain was still listed, but, as usual, did no teaching.

The major areas of study now include Chinese, Egyptian (though no courses were offered), Indic Studies, Semitics, and African Studies. The strategic and tactical importance of Africa in World War II was being felt. The emergence of African nations after the war demanded still more attention. But aside from the purely contemporary interests in Africa, something else was developing: an Afro-Asiatic school of linguistics, whereby connections were seen among language families of Africa and those in other parts of the Old World. The departmental requirements of both French and German, as well as Latin and Greek for certain courses, and for at least eight semester credits of undergraduate Hebrew shows

---

[3] Danby's magnum opus is his annotated translation of the Mishna (1933). I once asked him in Jerusalem what he considered the most pervasive principle in the Mishna. Without a moment's hesitation, he replied: "abhorrence of corpses."

that there was still adherence to the "old standards." The attenuation of such language requirements on the American scene between then and now is a facet of the considerable change that has affected all Semitics departments at home and abroad. These changes anticipated the coming of computers in ways that are not always understood. For example, the very useful publication of texts in translation (first of Latin and Greek, then of ancient Near Eastern texts in cuneiform, hieroglyphs, and alphabetic scripts) conveyed the impression that it was no longer necessary to learn the sources. "It is all translated!" Other valuable books, such as the Kittel Bible (which pulls out some of the "plums" from the evidence of the ancient translations and lists them in the footnotes), went hand in hand with the notion that it was not really necessary to read the Septuagint, Vulgate, Peshitta, or Targums, because whatever was of value in them was summed up in the footnotes of the Kittel Bible. The seminars of biblical philogians like Montgomery and Margolis met around long tables covered with books in Hebrew, Greek, Latin, and numerous oriental languages. Nowadays, the Kittel Bible is often all the "good" student needs; the mediocre student is satisfied with English translations. Translations, compendia and computer printouts can be convenient aids but the real scholars must control their fields from the sources.

The above comments are not intended as criticism but rather as descriptive of what has been happening. The newer trends often have advantages of another kind. There is no doubt that concern with textual criticism and linguistic minutiae can make it difficult for students to maintain perspective, whereas emancipation from details can give them more time to reckon with generalities. But, when the chips are down, what counts most in solid scholarship is direct control of the primary sources.

Harris continued to offer Modern Hebrew, but his real concern was reflected more in his course, "Analysis of a Near East Language Learned from a Native Informant." Speiser announced first-year Akkadian, but the other assyriological offerings were "omitted in 1943–44." Actually, Speiser's oncampus activity had given way to his Washington commitments connected with the war effort. Other courses "omitted in 1943–44" reflected the suspension of much of the department's purely intellectual concerns. Consigned to the backburner were: oriental history and culture, Hittite, comparative Semitic linguistics, Islamic religion, South Arabic, Ethiopic, Assyrian annals, and mythological, religious, and legal texts in Akkadian. On the other hand, African studies was represented by intensive courses on three modern languages offered by Harris, to wit, Moroccan Arabic, Hausa, and Swahili.

The picture remained much the same in 1944–45 (though without mention of the two lecturers). It is worth noting that Harris now offered only modern languages (Hebrew, Moroccan Arabic, Hausa, and Swahili)

and linguistics courses. Levi della Vida was responsible for classical
Arabic, Syro-Aramaic, Semitic epigraphy, and biblical Hebrew. Speiser
was listed for teaching Akkadian and sharing the responsibility for teaching an Old Testament book. It was a period of federal support for modern
dialects in a global war, with little encouragement for basic scholarship.
Overseas and especially Washington assignments siphoned off the human
resources (students and faculty) from the campus. Space does not permit
me to list the para-academic activities during the war years.

The academic year 1945–46 began with World War II over on both
fronts but the effects of war on academia lingered on. Offerings remained
much the same as in the preceding year. Speiser's return to teaching
biblical Hebrew and a seminar in Hurrian or Elamite and his disengage-
ment from Washington constituted the most significant development.

The academic year 1946–47 marks the beginning of the postwar revival
of learning. The faculty was now enriched by the new lecturer, Samuel
Noah Kramer. Kramer took his Ph.D. at Penn in 1930, writing his thesis
on the verbal system in the Nuzi tablets under the direction of Speiser.[4]
Destined to become a specialist in Sumerian literary texts, he studied
during the 1930s under Chiera and especially Arno Peobel at the University of Chicago's Oriental Institute. It was particularly under Poebel that
Kramer got his headstart in Sumerology. Penn can take pride in its role in
this regard: Poebel had been at Penn, Chiera was trained at Penn and
had served on the Penn faculty before going to Chicago, and Kramer
received his training for the doctorate at the University of Pennsylvania.
It was Kramer who now (1946–47) offered Sumerian.

With the war over, there were other signs of a return to normalcy. The
departmental staff resumed its course "Interconnections of Oriental Civilizations." However, wartime interests left its effects. Speiser now offered
"Recent History of the Near East." Though Moroccan Arabic, Hausa,
and Swahili were no longer listed, Harris taught Modern Hebrew, a
subject destined to grow in importance with the establishment of the
State of Israel in 1948.

Levi della Vida offered Arabic and Islamic history and religion; Speiser
taught the courses on Akkadian, including a seminar on the Nuzi Tablets,
as well as a seminar on either Hurrian or Elamite. Semitic epigraphy,
comparative Semitic grammar, biblical Hebrew and Aramaic were again
offered by the veteran staff of Levi della Vida, Speiser, and Harris. The
assignment of courses with small or zero enrollment to two or more
teachers made it possible to divide the teaching load equitably after
registration. The "veterans" were products of a tradition that enabled all
of them to handle Hebrew, Syro-Aramaic, and Arabic, in addition to their

[4]The title is *The Verb in the Kirkuk Tablets* (University of Pennsylvania, 1931; published
in Annual of the American Schools of Oriental Research 11 [1929–30].

specialties. No significant changes in faculty or offerings were made in 1946–47. The omission of Syriac was not of major significance, since it is linguistically almost the same as Aramaic.

The courses in 1947–48 were much the same as the preceding year. However, the chairman was now Speiser. Separated from his Washington connections and chairing the department, he was now in full charge of Penn's Semitic tradition and would so remain for the rest of his life (he died in 1965), which covered another decade and a half. His staff consisted of Professors Brown, Levi della Vida, Harris, and Kramer.

It should be noted that Kramer, who had succeeded Leon Legrain as the Clark Professor of Assyriology, also did some teaching, although he was immersed in piecing together the fragments of Sumerian literature in the University Museum.[5] Harris, whose interests were veering away from Semitics in the direction of linguistic science, still offered Modern Hebrew.

Giorgio Levi della Vida is memorable as a personality as well as a scholar. He once told me that about 30 percent of the words in the great native Arabic lexica never really existed but were the creations of the lexicographers who identified the letters of words in manuscripts incorrectly. In standard Arabic script, for example, the same letter is *b* (with an inferior dot), *t* (with two superior dots), *th* (with three superior dots), *n* (with a superior dot), *y* (with two inferior dots), and with a hamza the same letter stands for *alif*. (In other Arabic scripts, notably Kufic, the situation is still worse.) Scribal laxity or even flyspecks have thus given rise to new "words" in the lexica.

As an elegant Italian gentleman, he could be fastidious and react strongly to situations that offended his sensibilities. This did not happen often, but under the following extraordinary circumstances, I had occasion to observe it. In 1947 my wife and I were invited to attend an international conference on Islam at Princeton University. As a distinguished Islamist, Levi della Vida was an honored participant. We were all lodged in the Princeton Inn. Arriving in the lobby at about the same time, my wife and I told Giorgio we wanted to unpack in our room, and we suggested that he do likewise and that we all come down again in a few minutes for tea together. Mrs. Levi della Vida was still in Italy, and therefore Giorgio had to share a room with some other participant. When he came down, he looked unhappy, and I asked him what was wrong. He replied that his roommate was Ananda Coomaraswamy (the famous Indologist of the Boston Museum of Fine Arts). I inquired: "What's bad about that?" He retorted: "I found him sitting naked on his bed, contemplating his navel." Since no Venetian gentleman can be expected to put up with

---

[5] One of his students, Edmund Irwin Gordon, wrote an important thesis, on *Sumerian Proverbs and their Cultural Significance*, (University of Pennsylvania, 1955). An early death terminated his career.

such exotic "nonsense," Giorgio complained at the desk and was moved to another room where he was billeted with a more conventional Islamist. From what I knew of Coomaraswamy, he was not the navel-contemplating type. I suspect he was putting on an act to get rid of his roommate and have the room to himself. After the shocking complaint of Levi della Vida, the management could scarcely risk putting anyone else in Ananda's room. That the Indologist was hell-bent on outraging as many participants as possible was clear during the sessions. He got up and said, in the presence of several American missionaries from India, that Islam was tolerant as contrasted with the Christianity that the missionaries present were spreading. The fur flew until Coomaraswamy broke up the meeting by baring his teeth and yelling at Professor Christy Wilson (a missionary on the faculty of Princeton Theological Seminary): "You ought to be ashamed of your religion!" Such an enfant terrible was hardly suitable as a bedfellow for the elegant Giorgio Levi della Vida.

On returning to Italy, Giorgio was interviewed by the press. Like many upperclass, intellectual, Italian men, Georgio did not spend time practicing his religion, nor did he believe in its tenets. Though he was Jewish, his wife was a Catholic Italian noblewoman. One of the reporters asked Giorgio: "Professor, is it true that you have converted to Catholicism and forsaken the faith of your fathers?" "By no means!" replied Giorgio; "I have never left the faith of my fathers." "And, what is that faith?" asked the reporter. "Unbelief," answered Giorgio laconically.

Although both Giorgio and I worked in Philadelphia, we found Princeton more congenial. My wife Joan and I resided with our children in Princeton, and Giorgio often visited friends there. Joan and I planned a party in Giorgio's honor, and to make the occasion worthy of such a charming savant, we got up an impressive guest list limited to accomplished scholars of exceptional merit. Princeton is the kind of community where this is possible. All of the guests were aware of their own stature and insisted on talking. Nobody was willing to listen. The soiree was a failure socially. The Gordons learned an important lesson: for every genius that insists on talking, there must be at least one mediocrity willing to listen.

Georgio loved to tell anecdotes, but I soon discovered that he narrated them better than he listened to them. Several times I tried to tell him real "humdingers" only to see him frown and wrinkle his forehead over his bushy eyebrows that came together on the bridge of his nose. Then he would remark something like: "Your story goes back to a thirteenth century manuscript from Baghdad." I would have been happier with a lusty belly laugh but instead I always got a learned colophon in deadly earnest. So I stopped trying to entertain him with my stories, and instead I let him entertain me with his.

He was a truly cultivated Italian in the Renaissance tradition. If one misquoted Dante in some trivial detail, Giorgio would correct that person immediately. Although he was a generalist of the old school, he was at the same time a meticulous savant attuned to the best in twentieth century scholarship.

He had two daughters and only one son. The latter disappointed Giorgio, who expected any son of his to be a scholar. Instead, he was a champion tennis player. One day, when Giorgio complained to me about his son, who was an athlete instead of an academician, I asked him: "But hasn't he ever brought you any satisfaction?" "Yes, once," replied Giorgio with a wry smile. "I was returning to Italy from a trip abroad, and was entering customs at Rome, where an inspector was giving everyone a hard time, removing every article from every bag. But noticing the name tag on my valise, the inspector looked at me and inquired:

'Any relation to that great tennis player?'

'He is my son,' admitted Giorgio.

Said the inspector: 'Go right through, sir. It is an honor to be of service to the father of so famous a man!'"

6. THE SPEISER YEARS

Changes were visible in 1948–49. Speiser, the chairman, had on his staff Professors Brown, Harris, and Kramer; Visiting Professor Ranke was back; Associate Professor Franz Rosenthal had replaced Levi della Vida who had returned to his native Italy now that Fascism was gone; and the roster was completed by Assistant Professor Francis Rue Steele, Instructor Ernest Bender, and visiting Lecturer Mark Dresden.

The majors were Indic and Iranian Studies, Near Eastern and African Studies, and Chinese Studies.

Dresden brought back Avestan and introduced elementary Persian. "Persian" had come to mean the modern language of Islamic Iran. In the post–World War II period, no apology had to be made for listing this non-Semitic language in the same department that fostered Semitics. The concept of Islamics was now in the air and it was only a matter of time before Penn would house a whole Islamic institute devoted to Arabic, Persian, and Turkish. Egyptian, which had lain dormant, was now fully revived under Ranke once more, with three courses in Pharaonic Egyptian and another in Coptic.

Penn was fortunate in maintaining a succession of fine Arabists. Rosenthal was worthy of filling the shoes of Levi della Vida not only in Arabic but in Northwest Semitic as well. Speiser offered an array of his familiar courses, and, if overburdened, he had Steele to take over first-year Akkadian. The staff offered "Interconnections of Oriental Civilizations," while Speiser offered a three-year cycle on ancient Near Eastern history and culture. Kramer not only offered his course on Sumerian texts but also another entitled "Creative Writing in the Ancient Near East: a Comparative Literature of pre-biblical literatures of Egypt, Canaan, Hittite, Akkadian, and particularly of the Sumerians." The subtitle of the latter reflects Kramer's special love for Sumer. He had a broad training, but for him, although all the mentioned cultures had value, it was Sumerian alone that had "particular" significance. If any scholar has to have a "favorite child" to love, Sumerian is a good choice.

Ranke elected to return to Germany now that the war was over. Penn was fortunate in another accomplished Egyptologist from Germany to replace him; namely, Rudolf Anthes, who continued to offer more or less the same four language courses as well as a lecture course on Egyptian culture.[1]

[1] Professor Anthes trained two productive Egyptologists at Penn. The first was Henry

In 1950–51 the staff consisted of Speiser, as chairman, Professors Bodde, Brown, Harris, and Kramer; Visiting Professor Anthes; Associate Professor Rosenthal; and Assistant Professors Bender, Dresden, and Steele.

Dresden gave two courses on Persian as well as Old Persian and Avestan. He also offered Middle Persian (Pahlavi), which bridges the gap between the fall of the Achaemenian Empire toward the close of the fourth century B.C. and the Islamic conquest in the seventh century A.D. Since this covers the period when Parthian Iran "divided the world" with Rome and then when Sasanian Iran ruled the Babylonia of the Talmud and vied with Byzantium in ruling the Near East, Middle Iranian is important for several fields. The Semitics and cuneiform offerings remained much the same, though it might be noted that the only Hebrew offering is now Speiser's "A Book of the Bible." It is curious that all the modern Arabic and Hebrew courses have vanished, in spite of the flourishing future in store for them. This omission in 1950–51 is attributable to the fewness of the teachers, which was rendered the more acute because Harris had just about pulled out of Semitics. Rosenthal alone was responsible for Northwest Semitic, Arabic, South Arabic, an Islamic seminar, and Ugaritic, as well as Semitic epigraphy. Comparative Semitic grammar was announced as offered by Speiser, Rosenthal, or Harris.

The announcement for 1951 lists the faculty as follows:

Speiser, Professor of Semitics, Chairman

Rudolf Anthes, Professor of Egyptology and Curator of Egyptology in the University Museum

Zellig S. Harris, Professor of Linguistics

Samuel Noah Kramer, Clark Research Professor in Assyriology

Franz Rosenthal, Professor of Arabic

Mark J. Dresden, Assistant Professor of Iranian Languages and Civilization

Francis Rue Steele, Assistant Professor of Assyriology.

Kramer, in addition to his Sumerian seminar, taught undergraduate Hebrew. The emphasis of the department was solidly graduate, and if undergraduates were promising, they would (as in former years) be allowed to take some of the graduate courses. The demand for Hebrew on the part of Jewish undergraduates was satisfied in part by extracurricular study, both on and off campus. It should be noted that Anthes and Speiser teamed up to offer a course entitled "Introduction to Ancient

George Fischer, whose Ph.D. thesis was *Denderah in the Old Kingdom and its Aftermath* (University of Pennsylvania, 1955). Fischer is now the curator of the Egyptian section at the Metropolitan Museum of Art in New York City. The second was Alan Richard Schulman, whose doctoral dissertation was *Military Rank, Title and Organization in the Egyptian New Kingdom* (University of Pennsylvania, 1962). Schulman teaches on the Queens College Campus, City University of New York.

Egyptian and Mesopotamian History." No one staff member was skilled in both Egypt and the cuneiform world.

During the next couple of years, there were no major changes. A plethora of courses were listed, far more than the staff could actually teach simultaneously.

The academic year 1954–55 marked the introduction of South Asian Regional Studies as a separate department chaired by Professor Brown. Though in itself a significant innovation, it has no bearing on our subject, the Semitic tradition at the University of Pennsylvania. Oriental studies in 1954–55 was chaired by Speiser and staffed by Professors Anthes, Kramer, and Rosenthal, and Assistant Professors Dresden and Greenberg. Harris was no longer listed under Oriental Studies but, as Professor of Linguistics, was in the latter department. Dr. Moshe Greenberg,[2] trained by Speiser, was in charge of Hebrew instruction including postbiblical Hebrew literature. The veteran staff continued the accustomed courses with some omissions such as Ethiopic.

In 1956–57, a serious gap was created by the departure of Rosenthal for Yale University, with the result that no instruction was provided for Arabic, Islamic, Syro-Aramaic, Northwest Semitic or Semitic epigraphy. The chairman, Speiser, succeeded in getting an endowment transferred from Temple University to Penn, so that Speiser's new title was the A. M. Ellis Professor of Hebrew and Semitic Languages and Literatures. Dresden was now Research Professor of Iranian Languages. Otherwise things remained much the same. Kramer offered a course, "The Mythologies of the Ancient Near East," based on J. B. Pritchard's *Ancient Near Eastern Texts Relating to the Old Testament*. Greenberg's Hebrew courses (elementary and intermediate) were listed in the college (but not the graduate school) *Bulletin*. The Ellis family was primarily concerned with Hebrew at the undergraduate level, and so Greenberg's appointment was mainly to fill this need.

In 1957–58 Speiser was on leave, and H. L. Ginsberg took his place as Visiting Ellis Professor. Rosenthal's place was taken by another outstanding Arabist, professor S. D. Goitein. The veterans were Professors Kramer and Anthes. Kramer, in addition to his Sumerian seminar, continued to offer his lecture courses on creative writing, and on mythologies of the ancient Near East, while Anthes offered three levels of ancient Egyptian, a course on Coptic, and an introduction to ancient Egyptian art and archaeology. Ginsberg offered a course each on Isaiah, Northwest Semitic, and Ugaritic. Goitein taught first and second year Arabic in addition to one on Islamic history, plus his Islamic seminar.

[2]Greenberg's thesis, *The HAB/PIRU* (University of Pennsylvania, 1954) deals with the cApiru, a people spread throughout the ancient Near East and mentioned in cuneiform sources during the second millennium B.C. Their name is often identified with "Hebrews."

Greenberg, who had a particular interest in Ezekiel Kaufmann's writings on Old Testament religion (some of which he translated into English), offered a course, "Studies in the Religion of Israel." The faculty shifts necessitated the suspension of instruction in South Arabic, Ethiopic, Hittite, Hurrian, and comparative Semitic grammar.

Speiser returned in 1958–59, and among his varied courses, Hittite was restored. On the other hand, Aramaic was added to the list of subjects that had been temporarily suspended. It should be observed that scholars such as Goitein and Speiser were experienced in Aramaic; it is simply impossible for any scholar to function in everything at the same time.

Moshe Greenberg was now Associate Professor of Hebrew and offered postbiblical Hebrew literature. Modern Hebrew as well as modern Arabic disappeared from the offerings, although by this time their revival and growth were foregone conclusions. Dresden, Goitein, Kramer, and Speiser continued to offer their old standbys.

It should be mentioned that Kramer's interest in mythologies of the world was expressed in the form of a symposium in Mexico City in 1959, which was held in conjunction with the American Anthropological Association. Kramer handled the Sumerian side and invited guest lecturers to cover their respective specialities. Anthes covered Egypt; Hans C. Güterbock, the Hittites; Michael H. Jameson, Greece; Dresden, Iran; C. H. Gordon, Canaan; and so forth. The lectures appeared as chapters of a book entitled *Mythologies of the Ancient World* edited by Kramer (New York: Anchor Books, Doubleday, 1961).

The academic year 1959–60 witnessed no significant changes. Among former offerings now dropped, is postbiblical Hebrew literature. The same holds for 1960–61. In the latter year, Dresden is listed among the resident faculty as usual, though all the Persian courses are listed only as to be given in subsequent years.

Two new faces were added in 1961–62: the Far Eastern archaeologist, Associate Professor Schuyler W. R. Cammann (Chinese Studies), and Assistant Professor Svi Rin. Dr. Rin was a skilled and dedicated Hebraist specializing in biblical Hebrew and Ugaritic. His spoken Hebrew was not only his native speech, but exceptional for its purity. Among his accomplishments were masterful translations from English into Hebrew. The undergraduate *Bulletin* for 1961–62 reflects Greenberg and Rin sharing the Hebrew program. The presence of two full-time faculty members whose primary responsibility was undergraduate Hebrew, anticipated the burgeoning of Hebrew courses to come in the years ahead.

In the *Announcement* for 1962–63, Anthes appears for the last time, marking another serious break in the continuity of Egyptology at Penn.

In 1963–64, Visiting Professor Richard Ettinghausen enhanced the program by giving "Islamic Art and Architecture" on which he was an outstanding authority.

All through these years, Speiser remained the chairman and was responsible for appointments and other matters of consequence. However, his health was deteriorating, and he was not to live much longer. Greenberg was soon to depart for Hebrew University in Jerusalem. Speiser continued to the end to represent Akkadian and Old Testament studies, so that his death in 1965 would leave gaping voids and end an era at Penn. Anthes was also nearing the end of his life.

Changes were inevitable in 1965–66, some of which were of a transitory nature, for visiting faculty were called in. The void in Egyptian was filled by William Kelley Simpson as visiting professor in Egyptology and curator of the Egyptian section in the University Museum.[3] He was assisted by David O'Connor, A.B., as instructor of Egyptology, who offered "Introduction to Egyptian Archaeology." Joseph A. Fitzmeyer, S.J., served as visiting lecturer on West Semitic linguistics and offered Northwest Semitic and Ugaritic.

As early as 1965, plans were laid at Penn to establish a Middle Eastern center focusing on the modern Islamic scene. Funding under the National Defense Education Act and initial grants from the Ford Foundation enabled the center to grow rapidly. By 1967 the director was appointed: Dr. Thomas Naff.

The demise of Speiser and the establishment of the Middle East Center and its spin-off, the Middle East Research Center, are not unrelated. Although Speiser was involved during World War II with federal operations, his basic commitment was to "classical" Semitic and cuneiform learning. He was a strong, even dictatorial, leader, who understandably saw in postwar pressures an encroachment on purely academic orientation.

The establishment, through federal and foundational subsidies of area centers, including Middle East centers, was very much in the air. Support for purely academic programs was meager compared with the sums available for such centers. Facts and figures bore out concerns about the possibility of the tail wagging the dog.

The Middle East centers were concerned with the modern scene and primarily intended to serve businesses and governments. In the decade following the oil crisis of 1973, the spotlight was on the Middle East more than ever before, and Saudi Arabian oil seemed far more important than the Qur'an and all of the Muslim classics. Centers for modern Arabic, Persian, and Turkish language and area studies needed no justification.

---

[3] He is now professor of Egyptology at Yale University and curator of the Egyptian and Near Eastern section of the Boston Museum of Fine Arts.

The trouble arose from affiliating such centers with classical learning in the university colleges and graduate schools. Furthermore, the presence of Hebrew among the Middle East languages and areas touched off an ideological confrontation between the Hebrew and Arabic curricula. All concerned tended to deny special interests. But the special interests were real and the denials convinced nobody.

I would like to insert a personal note. At Brandeis University I was in charge of Mediterranean Studies, which included Arabic and Hebrew. To preclude any political heat, I followed a simple rule: "nothing after Napoleon." In this way Jewish and Muslim students who were interested in objective scholarship studied side by side and were happy to cultivate each other's heritage as well as their own. If a Semitics department keeps out of modern politics and economics, it can retain its classical and objective character. And if area centers fulfill their mission without hiding behind the skirts of classical departments for "academic respectability," there is room for both on the campus of a large university.

Ephraim Avigdor Speiser was a precocious scholar of ancient Near Eastern studies. He was born in Poland, and his adolescence was fraught with hardship, including digging trenches in World War I. He never got over his underprivileged youth and those who knew him well felt the overcompensating aggressiveness during his later, academically successful years.

After coming to Philadelphia, he took his Ph.D. at Dropsie College under Max Margolis who trained him in Old Testament philology and Septuagint research. At the same time, Speiser availed himself of the resources at the University of Pennsylvania, including contact with Edward Chiera who inducted him into Nuzi studies. Chiera's departure from Penn to the Oriental Institute at the University of Chicago created an opening at the University of Pennsylvania for Speiser. There he rapidly rose to the rank of full professor and also gained the directorship of the expedition at Tell Billa and Tepe Gawra.

Speiser's careful philology and linguistic training were necessary for correcting the more casual approach of George Barton. Speiser did not hesitate to criticize Barton (and others) in class. That Speiser was in general a better cuneiformist, Semitist, and teacher than Barton does not tell the whole story. Barton, for example, had at least a bowing acquaintance with Egyptology—which Speiser lacked, to the detriment of his Anchor Bible Commentary on Genesis, for Genesis is replete with Egyptian influence.

Though I respected Speiser's gifts as a savant and teacher, he took a dislike to me and, while denying any prejudice or animosity, proved to be the most damaging professional enemy of my entire career. I left an instructorship at Penn to go into the field where I began to work with Speiser in 1931–32 at Billa and Gawra. In the evenings, we read Chiera's published corpus of Nuzi tablets. Those sessions got me started in Nuzi studies. As far as I can tell, it was my following in his footsteps in Nuzi scholarship—including the biblical parallels—that kindled his ire against me. I have always felt pleased when a student emulates me and walks in my footsteps, but Speiser was resentful and jealous. He wanted me to work on Aramaic incantations *instead*. I indeed kept working on those incantations, but not *instead* of Assyriology.

I continued to look up to Speiser throughout most of 1931–32, until I made the mistake of asking his advice on a project that I wanted to undertake: a beginner's manual of Akkadian based exclusively on Hammurapi's laws. He forbade me to undertake it because "only a senior scholar should write an elementary textbook in any field." I still think his advice was wrong, but since I had sought his advice, I was loath to flout it. That was the last time I sought a superior's advice on any project I wished to undertake.

Until 1935 I remained in the field, whereas Speiser returned to the University of Pennsylvania in 1932, where he sat on the committee of the American Schools of Oriental Research. There he gradually had my salary reduced to zero and saw to it that the instructorship I had left to work with him in the field was given to a rival who, though talented, systematically flattered Speiser and used the job as a stepping stone, which he abandoned as soon as possible. Fortunately, Albright disliked Speiser, and made a point of protecting me from the professional destruction that Speiser had planned.

It would be a mistake to insist that Speiser behaved toward me as he did because of all humankind he hated only me. Another student who later studied under him wanted to work on Sumerian literature with Speiser's colleague Kramer. Speiser absolutely forbade the student to do so. The student, after receiving the doctorate, got out of Speiser's clutches by taking a post at the University of Chicago. Meanwhile, his Sumerian dreams had been killed—like my Akkadian primer. Speiser was a bully and, in a small country with more limited professional opportunities than the United States, might have succeeded in killing off every able young scholar in whom he detected any spirit of independence.

He was a remarkable linguist at all levels—whether in dealing with ancient texts or conversing in modern dialects. His English was excellent. He spoke and read German and French as well as a number of Slavic languages. He was also fluent in Arabic and Hebrew. He could turn on a lot of charm. He was skilled at kissing up and kicking down.

His health was not good—as was obvious during the 1931–32 campaign in Iraq. Yet, although he was dyspeptic, he insisted on unduly fancy meals. He once summoned our Hindu cook to upbraid him for not serving a lunch with "*two* meat courses seasoned with *two* rich sauces."

Being short of stature, he had more than a touch of a Napoleonic complex. He bragged about his athletic prowess and general superiority—including his skill at table tennis. When his opponent beat him at this game, Speiser refused to talk to anyone for a full day. He had to be right in all things, great and small, and his arrogance left no room for anyone else's place in the sun.

But, when all is said and done, Speiser was an accomplished scholar and an outstanding teacher.[4] He was at the helm at Penn during a period when academic standards were threatened by a government-sponsored spirit of immediacy. When the chips were down, he upheld scientific scholarship even while cancer was relentlessly ending his life. Whatever serious classroom training I got in Assyriology, I owe to him.

[4]Among the Ph. D. dissertations written under Speiser's supervision were several on the Nuzi tablets. Two were published in 1937: one by Moshe Berkooz, *The Nuzi Dialect of Akkadian: Orthography and Phonology* (published in *Language,* dissertation 23, the Linguistic Society of America) and the other by Dorothy Cross, *Movable Property in the Nuzi Documents* (published in *American Oriental Series* 10). In 1936 two theses (by MacRae and Purves) were submitted, later to be incorporated in the important book by Ignace J. Gelb, Pierre M. Purves, and Allan A. MacRae, *Nuzi Personal Names* (Chicago: University of Chicago; Oriental Institute Publications 57 [1943]). MacRae covered the Akkadian and Sumerian elements and Purves, the non-Semitic (especially the Hurrian) elements.

7. THE CURRENT SCENE

The 1966–67 undergraduate *Bulletin* has Greenberg occupying the A. M. Ellis Professorship of Hebrew and Semitic Languages and Literatures with the rank of professor. Now that Speiser was dead and Brown was retired, there was a break in the leadership. Young instructors with no graduate degrees appeared: Henry Toledano, A.B., to assist Goitein; and Barry Eichler, A.B. (to become one of the mainstays in Hebrew and Assyriology),[1] and David O'Connor, A.B., in Egyptology (eventually to become the mainstay of Egyptian archaeology). May Lou Green was the instructor for Turkish. For the fall semester, a distinguished Egyptologist, J. Černý, offered a course on Egyptian culture. The trouble with small departments is that there is no backup, somewhat like a baseball team with only one pitcher, one catcher, four infielders and three outfielders. The loss or indisposition of one scholar creates a breakdown in the operation. Therefore, courses such as South Arabic, Ethiopic, Hurrian, and so forth, could not be offered.

An important addition to the faculty in 1967–68 is Professor Åke Sjöberg in Assyriology, who succeeded Kramer upon the latter's retirement in 1968 to the Clark Chair and the curatorship in the museum. Kramer was dedicated to Sumerian, and it is appropriate that his successor has built up at the University of Pennsylvania the most important Sumerological project on the world scene today: the Sumerian Dictionary Project. There is no satisfactory Sumerian dictionary yet in existence. The task is enormous but Sjöberg has the files, the staff, and, above all, the knowledge and capability of launching the project. The first volume, covering only the letter *b*, appeared in 1984. It shows that the project is well-conceived and well-handled. The only unfortunate aspect of the project is that each fascicle requires a great expenditure of time and labor. This means decades, not merely years, and by the time half the fascicles appear, the early ones will be out of date. This is no reason for not giving the project high priority. The most useful tool in Assyriology is the Chicago Assyrian Dictionary (CAD), which has been in progress for over half a century and is still not completed. Yet no Assyriologist can move without referring to the fascicles that have appeared. Alas, nothing is perfect in this world!

[1] Barry Lee Eichler's doctorate was soon after awarded (*Nuzi Personal Ditennūtu Transactions and their Mesopotamian Analogues* [1967]).

The 1967–68 *Announcement* for graduate studies lists also James D. Muhly, A.B., as lecturer on ancient and Near Eastern history, who gave a course entitled, "Introduction to Mesopotamian History and Archaeology", while O'Connor offered instruction on Egyptian.

No significant change took place in 1968–69. But page 347 in the *University of Pennsylvania Bulletin: Graduate Studies 1968–69*, notes that the "Modern Near East Language and Area Center," established with the help of the United States Office of Education and with the cooperation of the Department of Political Science, is housed in this (Oriental Studies) Department. In other words, the center, whose program "stresses understanding the modern scene," is only "housed" in the Department of Oriental Studies. Islamic custom requires that a man with two wives has to provide separate housing for them. The housing of rivals with overlapping interests but with different aims, under one and the same roof, is not conducive to harmony.

The *Bulletin for Undergraduate Courses of Study for 1969–70* mentioned as instructor of introductory and intermediate Hebrew, Moshe Gil.[2] Greenberg was to leave Penn and join the faculty of Hebrew University in Jerusalem.

The *Bulletin for Graduate Studies, 1969–70*, named Arieh Loya as assistant professor of Arabic. Thomas Naff, the director of the Near East Center, as associate professor of Arabic gave the courses "History of the Ottoman Empire" and "Survey of Near Eastern History from the Rise of Islam"; he also directed "Readings in Modern Near Eastern History." Goitein was now in retirement, and the classical emphasis in Arabic Studies (from Jastrow to Goitein, through Montgomery, Levi della Vida, and Rosenthal) had made way for a more modern mood. Osman Tuna, as assistant professor, offered Turkish language and civilization.

Ties with the University Museum were strengthened in 1970–71 through three new names on the teaching staff: James B. Pritchard, curator of biblical archaeology in the museum, was now also Professor of Religious Thought, and Erle V. Leichty, curator of Akkadian language and literature in the museum, was also associate professor of Assyriology (later to become full professor and assistant director of the Sumerian Dictionary Project). Lanny Bell, B.A., was assistant in the Egyptian section of the museum and also instructor in Egyptology.[3] With Sjöberg as tenured Clark Professor of Assyriology and curator of the museum's

---

[2] Moshe Gil received his doctorate in 1970. His thesis is entitled *The Institution of Charitable Foundations in the Light of the Cairo Geniza Documents*. (He is now (1986) on the faculty of Bar Ilan University, engaged in preparing his fourth volume of Judeo-Arabic texts from the Cairo Geniza. Dr. Gil is thus following in the footsteps of his mentor, Professor Goitein).

[3] Bell received his Ph.D. in 1976, writing *Interpreters and Egyptianized Nubians in Ancient Egyptian Foreign Policy: Aspects of the History of Egypt and Nubia*.

tablet collection, four of the five teachers were on the museum staff, too. The only exception was Price Meade, B.A., M.A., instructor of Persian. And it was the four connected with the museum who constituted the foundation for reestablishing the department in the wake of the breakdown following Speiser's death.

The *Bulletin for the Undergraduate Courses of Study 1971–72* listed William Hanaway, assistant professor of Persian, as teaching first and second year Persian, as well as an introduction to Persian literature. The *Bulletin for Graduate Studies 1971–72* listed David Owen as a research associate in Assyriology, and assistant curator in the Department of Underwater Archaeology in the University Museum. Owen, while teaching Assyriology at Dropsie, was also working on cuneiform tablets at the museum. He was an accomplished underwater archaeologist, too, trained by George Bass. It was Bass who brought distinction to the University Museum in underwater archaeology but was lured away by Texas A & M. Owen, who had been trained in Assyriology at Brandeis University, became also a Sumerologist through contact particularly with Kramer at Penn. Dr. Owen soon left Philadelphia for Cornell where he is now a professor in Near Eastern history and archaeology. Assistant Professor Jeffrey H. Tigay obtained the Ellis chair for Hebrew. A new instructor in Hebrew also appeared: Neil H. Tannenbaum, B.A., LL.B.

The trend to establish links with anthropology was again expressed, this time with the appointment of Brian J. Spooner, M.A., D. Phil., as assistant professor of Near Eastern anthropology. Contemporary pressures account for the listing of Assistant Professor John C. Lambalet to offer in the fall term a course on "Operation and Performance of the Economics of the Near East, Including the Economics of Oil".

The *University of Pennsylvania Bulletin, Undergraduate Courses of Study 1972–73,* noted some changes. Tigay continued (as he does down to the present) to occupy the Ellis chair for Hebrew. Tigay also offered the course, "The Bible in Translation." Courses on the English Bible had once been a monopoly of the English Department; indeed it was a very popular lecture course given by Provost Josiah H. Penniman in my student days.

The *Bulletin* for graduate studies, 1972–73, listed the Near Eastern specialist Edward Hourani as adjunct professor. Barry Eichler was assistant professor of Assyriology and assistant curator of the tablet collection in the museum; he also offered a course on Rabbinic texts, specifically, readings in Tannaitic Halakic Midrash. Quite a few courses required no language skills, for example, courses on Turkey; the Arabs; Islamic art; religion, and history; Mesopotamian literature and culture; Old Testament; Egyptian history, culture, archaeology; and so forth. On pages 364–66, more than fifty courses were named as omitted in 1972–73. These sparse facts reflected several interlocked factors: the growth of modern Near Eastern studies (as exemplified in Penn's center), the resultant dilution of the classical Semitic tradition, and, most important of all, the times.

The *Bulletin, Undergraduate Courses of Study 1973–74*, had a new offering by Eichler: "Medieval Hebrew Literature: Biblical Exegesis" (fall semester) and "Legal Codes" (spring semester). It should perhaps be noted that "legal codes" in Judaica means something different from the same designation in biblical and ancient Near Eastern studies. For the ancient field it means law codes such as Hammurapi's and the legal sections of Exodus and Deuteronomy. In Judaica it includes systematizations of ritual and other aspects of religious life. Thus, when Assyriologists speak of "codes" they mean one thing; when medievalists in the Judaic field use the same word, they mean something else.

The *Bulletin for Graduate Studies 1973–74* (page 331) again lists over fifty courses omitted in 1973–74. Omitting so many courses is a questionable procedure, but it has a certain positive implication: it reflects an intention to revive them.

In 1974–75 the undergraduate courses of study include "Dead Sea Scrolls" by Tigay. These texts are of prime importance at many levels. They provide us with copies of Old Testament books almost a thousand years earlier than the oldest copies of Hebrew biblical books known previous to the Dead Sea discoveries, made shortly after World War II. One of the revelations of these texts is that they show more variations than the Hebrew Bibles current in recent centuries. In the days of Montgomery and Margolis, it was an axiom that each book of the Bible started out as a pristine, pure original, and through scribal errors, different schools of texts were developed. The Dead Sea Scrolls showed that, to the contrary, the uniformity familiar to us was usually imposed on an earlier diversity. In fact, it was the diversity that forced the authorities around 100 A.D. (i.e., between the destruction of Jerusalem in 70 A.D. and the Bar Kokhba rebellion in 132–135 A.D.) to end the chaos of textual variations by establishing a uniform textus receptus. The scrolls also portrayed a kind of sectarian Judaism about which we knew too little previously. And the sectarians preserved many apocryphal and pseudepigraphical books, some of them completely new to us. It is worth calling attention to this, because it is from such courses that the spirit of keeping up with new discoveries was maintained at Penn during a critical period of changing times.

The *Bulletin* graduate studies 1974–75 listed a course on the Mishna, highlighting the beginnings of postbiblical Hebrew poetry and midrash, by Judah Goldin, who came to Penn from Yale to serve as professor of postbiblical Hebrew literature.

The undergraduate courses of study for 1975–76 included language courses on Akkadian and Hebrew. The Sanskritist Ludo Rocher was chairman. Rin handled Modern Hebrew; Tigay, Old Testament; and Goldin, rabbinics. The Arabic offerings included modern Arabic. Cultural courses, with no language requirement, dealt with Turkey, the Islamic Near East, Anatolia, ancient Israel, Mesopotamia, Egypt, and Iran.

The *Bulletin* for graduate studies for 1975–76 no longer required a reading knowledge of both French and German, but only one of them; this reflected a nationwide tendency toward the reduction of language requirements.

The subjects officially offered were now listed as follows: cuneiform studies (especially Sumerian and Akkadian), Egyptian, biblical and postbiblical studies, Hebrew, Iranian (i.e., pre-Islamic), Arabic, Persian (i.e., Islamic), Turkish and Near Eastern studies in a discipline of the student's choice (e.g., literature, linguistics, etc.).

In 1976–77 George Makdisi became chairman. Schuyler W. R. Cammann, now a professor of history, offered lecture courses on Islamic art and architecture. Leichty and Muhly offered courses on ancient near eastern history and archaeology.

The undergraduate offerings for 1977–78 listed Associate Professor David O'Connor as giving the courses on Egyptology, while Rin's Hebrew courses now extended to Old Testament too.

The *Bulletin, Information for Graduate Studies, 1977–78* listed Rin as teaching also comparative Semitic grammar, Northwest Semitic, and Syriac; Sjöberg taught Sumerian; Muhly, Hittite; and both Leichty and Eichler gave Akkadian courses. Both O'Connor and Bell gave Egyptian courses while Assistant Professor Nash taught Hebrew. Thus, 1977–78 marked a return toward the classical Semitic tradition.

The *Bulletin, Undergraduate Courses of Study for 1979–80,* listed a large number of survey courses with no language requirement. The *Bulletin, Information for Graduate Studies, 1979–80,* initiated a new course called "Practicum in Teaching." This was described as supervised preparation of material and class presentation within the framework of an existing course dealing with the student's major interest of concentration. Arabic courses were offered by Professor George Makdisi, Associate Professor Roger M. A. Allen, and Assistant Professor Adnan Haydar. Associate Professor Hanaway offered both classical (= medieval) and modern Persian.

The *Bulletin, Information for Graduate Studies 1980–81* listed both Associate Professor David B. O'Connor and Dr. David P. Silvermann as teaching Egyptology. O'Connor handled the instruction of history and of artifacts, while Silvermann taught Egyptian language, including Coptic. Rin now offered also Ugaritic. An innovation was Armenian language taught by Oshagn and Stone. Although Armenian is Indo-European, it is a language of some influence in the Semitic Near East. For example, the

Armenian Bible is a daughter translation of the Greek Bible. In the days of intensive textual criticism of the Old Testament, scholars like Margolis and Montgomery would reckon with Armenian in their attempt to restore the original Septuagint, and talented graduate students, without the benefit of courses in Armenian would learn enough of the language to collate the Armenian and Greek texts accurately.

In 1981–82, Nazih Daher was among the instructors of Arabic. Colloquial Arabic was included in the curriculum. With the retirement of Dresden, Old Persian and Avestan had vanished. The Persologist, William Hanaway, who dealt with Islamic Persian, fully appreciated the importance of the older pre-Islamic stages of the language and assured me that he would see to it that a replacement would be appointed for Old Persian, Avestan, and Pahlavi. (The *Graduate Academic Bulletin, 1983–1985* soon after announced the revival of Old Persian and Avestan.)

At the end of 1981–82, Rin retired as emeritus professor of Semitic studies. True to his reputation as a dedicated teacher, he continued to study with and guide students individually in his small but busy study in the university library.

In 1982–83, Associate Professor William L. Hanaway served as chairman, and Associate Professor Roger M. A. Allen served as undergraduate chairman. The place of Emeritus Professor Dresden (Old Persian and Avestan) had not yet been filled. However, Emeritus Professor Kramer not only had had good successors, but the Sumerian Dictionary Project has made of Penn the Sumerological "capital of the world."

The faculty was large. The list is too long to give in full, but here are the main names of those involved with the Semitic tradition: (1) Professors: Goldin, Leichty, Makdisi, Muhly, Sjöberg; (2) Adjunct Professor: Albert Hourani; (3) Associate Professors: M. A. Allen, Eichler, Hanaway, O'Connor, Tigay, Silvermann, and Irene Winter (history of art).

The proliferation of courses was unmistakable. No less than seventy-seven courses were listed for the Near East alone (i.e., not counting India, East Asia, etc.) in the undergraduate courses of study for 1982–83. To be sure, quite a few of them were without teachers to offer them, and it is difficult to estimate the student response. Assyriology, Egyptology, Hebrew, Arabic, Turkish, Persian, and a plethora of lecture courses were offered.

The graduate offerings were grouped under several headings: (1) ancient and modern culture, history, archaeology, and languages of the Near East from Egypt to Iran; (2) ancient, medieval, and modern Hebrew; (3) classical and modern Arabic; (4) Islamic Persian language and literature; and (5) Ottoman and modern Turkish.

The curriculum as a whole might convey the impression that oriental studies is in a state of flux. But a hard look at the dedicated individual scholars and the work they are doing with their students and in their research shows that Penn is alive and well.

Times have changed. There are more students, teachers, and courses than there were in the old pioneering days. Concern for the troubled present in a shrinking world has made inroads on the classical concerns of older generations. The knowledge explosion has curtailed perspective, but at the same time it has brought tighter controls and methods. The Semitic tradition at Penn is going forward, even though it is organizationally part of the Department of Oriental Studies, along with Indic, Chinese, Japanese, and Southeast Asian studies. The Modern Near East Center is not only housed in the same quarters as oriental studies, but the faculties and courses interpenetrate each other. This has its disadvantages; for example, Arabic and Hebrew, instead of being treated as sister Semitic languages that illuminate each other, tend to become polarized for political reasons. But there is something to be said for giant departments: when the crunch comes, it is the little departments that are picked off, and the big ones that survive.

The Semitic tradition at Penn is a century old. It has not merely survived but grown between the 1880s and the 1980s. My teacher, James A. Montgomery, was there on the ground floor as an undergraduate, class of '87. His life and mine span the entire century of Penn's tradition of Semitics. It started out creatively and goes on creatively, maintaining Penn's position in the forefront of the field.

DATE DUE

GAYLORD			PRINTED IN U.S.A.